The Healing Path

The Healing Path

A Memoir and an Invitation

JAMES FINLEY

ORBIS BOOKS
Maryknoll, New York 10545

Fourth Printing, May 2023

Founded in 1970, Orbis Books endeavors to publish works that enlighten the mind, nourish the spirit, and challenge the conscience. The publishing arm of the Maryknoll Fathers and Brothers, Orbis seeks to explore the global dimensions of the Christian faith and mission, to invite dialogue with diverse cultures and religious traditions, and to serve the cause of reconciliation and peace. The books published reflect the views of their authors and do not represent the official position of the Maryknoll Society. To learn more about Maryknoll and Orbis Books, please visit our website at www.orbis-books.com.

Manufactured in the United States of America.

Manuscript editing and typesetting by Joan Weber Laflamme.

Library of Congress Cataloging-in-Publication Data

Names: Finley, James, author.
Title: The healing path : a memoir and an invitation / James Finley.
Identifiers: LCCN 2022038381 (print) | LCCN 2022038382 (ebook) | ISBN 9781626985100 (trade paperback) | ISBN 9781608339723 (epub)
Subjects: LCSH: Finley, James. | Psychologists—United States—Biography. | Spiritual directors—United States—Biography.
Classification: LCC BF109.F56 A3 2023 (print) | LCC BF109.F56 (ebook) | DDC 150.19/5092 [B]—dc23/eng/20221123
LC record available at https://lccn.loc.gov/2022038381
LC ebook record available at https://lccn.loc.gov/2022038382

Contents

Acknowledgments

I am grateful to the following people whose encouragement, support and constructive criticism have significantly contributed to these reflections: Frank Sasinowski, Melody Goetz, Bonnie Badenoch, Jo Hadlock King, Mirabai Starr, Jack Finney, Diane Bunker, Don and Paige Marrs, Bob Weathers, Janna Gosselin, Tom Stella, William Brennan, Matt Mumber, Leigh Schickendantz, Donald Cozzens, and my daughters, Kelly Moorhead and Amy Finley.

Introduction

These reflections mark out a path, a way of life, in which we as human beings may be healed from all that hinders us from experiencing the steady, strong currents of divinity that flow on and on in the bittersweet alchemy of our lives. The surprising thing is that the intimate healing that spirituality brings into our lives is often hidden in the muck and mire of the very things about ourselves we wish were not true. The secret opening through which we pass into wholeness is hidden in the center of those wounds we are most afraid to approach. The door that grants access to boundless fulfillment is hidden in the unfinished business of our lives: the places where we do not want to feel vulnerable, the things we tend not to sit with or listen to, the sometimes sad, sometimes tender, sometimes disarmingly simple, sometimes joyful things that make up the intimate substance of who we really are and are called to be.

As I write this introduction I am immersed in these intimate depths, sitting next to my beloved wife, Maureen, as she lies here dying in the final stages of Alzheimer's. Even though she is unconscious and cannot open her eyes to look at me, I believe she can hear me as I speak from my heart in whispered words. Just now I told her that the waves of unbearable pain and crying that from time to time overtake me seem to soften at least a little as I learn to be more accepting of the immensity and mystery of her death. After all, immensity and mystery have woven our years together from the very start.

The slowness with which she is gently fading away from me seems continuous with the slow setting of the sun out over the ocean, which is just beyond this darkening room where Maureen and I have lived and shared so much over the past thirty years.

I just told her that my suffering in trying to imagine life without her is eased in sensing that her soul is already beginning to pass over into God, leaving but a long vapor trail of herself in which she is still barely tethered to her body.

Over the years Maureen and I would often share insights that came to us in our mornings, sitting here together in what we called our monastic silence. From time to time she might share a passage from one of her favorite writings, perhaps the essay in Thomas Merton's

Disputed Questions titled "A Philosophy of Solitude," or that lucid little commentary on Meister Eckhart, *The Way of Paradox*. I, in turn, might share a passage from the text of a mystic in which I was immersed at the time. Then we would return to our shared silent reading. It was such a sweet and subtle way to be so inexplicably one with each other in the presence of God. I suppose that I am now sitting here saying these things to her, knowing in my heart that she is listening from a depth of presence that I can scarcely imagine. I suppose too that I am sharing this with you as a way of inviting you to join us in these words, which are becoming our point of entry into the healing path this book explores.

I just now shared with Maureen a memory that I have shared with her many times over our years together. The memory is about how deeply affected I was by something Thomas Merton said to us novices not long after I had entered the cloistered Trappist monastery of the Abbey of Gethsemani in Kentucky. Merton, who was the master of novices, was speaking to us about an old lay brother who had just died. He encouraged us to realize that when we die, we do not go anywhere. We do not orbit the earth a few times and then take off for God in some far-off celestial realm. For as scripture tells us, "In God we live and move and have our being" (Acts 17:28). All the angels along with all the blessed who have crossed over into God are here with us in the vast interiority of God, in whom we subsist as light subsists in flame.

But we tend not to see the deathless presence of God. Nor do we tend to see the deathless presence of ourselves subsisting in God, breath by breath, heartbeat by heartbeat. I think this is what Jesus meant in telling us that we have eyes to see but do not see (Mk 8:18). Finally, we tend not to see the deathless mystery of ourselves, of others, and of all things, that alone is ultimately real. Hence the fear and confusion in which we lose our way in this life. It is in this traumatized incapacity to abide in our all-pervasive oneness that we act out the traumatizing things we do to ourselves, to others, and to the earth that sustains us. Thus, on the journey toward experiential self-knowledge our prayer becomes, "Lord, that I might see you in this and each passing moment of my life."

As I write these words, I know that the depth of presence and love they express is all-encompassing, vast, and true. But here is the painful, intimate thing. The density and intensity of the dread I feel in not knowing how I am going to be able to survive without Maureen closes off my ability to experience the consoling truths these words embody. In moments like this I have come to understand God as a Presence that protects us from nothing, even as we are inexplicably sustained in all things.

For several months now I have been stuck in not knowing how to begin the introduction to these reflections on the spirituality of healing. I had no way of knowing that I would begin in this way, sitting next to Maureen as she lay dying. But now it seems providentially appropriate that I begin by including you in this intimate exchange among Maureen, God, and myself. This is so because for the past thirty years Maureen and I have been aware of how deeply our relationship with each other has included our relationships with the men and women who have come to us for psychotherapy and spiritual direction. In endlessly varied ways our interactions with each other as husband and wife and with those coming to us for help have helped us to find our own way along the healing path. And so I am sharing these reflections in concert with my longstanding resonance with Maureen in the hope that what I am sharing with you here will help you to find your own way through the mysterious realms in which sorrow and joy merge with God's presence, carrying you forward into all your unknown tomorrows.

Of course, attempting to communicate such delicate matters in a book is not the same as a face-to-face encounter in which you could share your own experiences, ask questions, and share your own insights with me. But being with one another in the pages of this book has the advantage of allowing you to read these words in the same attentive manner in which I am writing them. Insofar as this occurs, I hope and trust that you might find here words of reassurance and guidance in your ongoing healing journey.

Know that the kinds of things I have been saying to Maureen embody the spiritual worldview of contemplative Christianity in which I was immersed in the nearly six years I lived in the monastery. During those years it was my good fortune to have Thomas Merton as my guide in the gentle art of contemplative living. From him I discovered that the mystical foundations of healing that contemplative living brings into our lives consist of learning how to seek, find, and give ourselves to God, who is wholly given to us in each passing moment of our lives.

When I left the monastery and began to lead weekend contemplative retreats in the United States and Canada, I spoke from the depths of my heart in an attempt to share with those present, as I will be sharing with you, that we do not have to live in a monastery to find our way into the deep healing and liberation that monastic life nurtures and protects. For this contemplative wisdom is present in the hidden recesses of our own bodies, minds, and hearts, waiting to be recognized, cultivated, and shared with others day by day.

Know, too, that while I will be turning primarily to passages in the writings of Thomas Merton and related sources in the mystical lineage of my own Christian tradition, I will also be drawing on the timeless wisdom that is present in the contemplative traditions of all the world's great religions and that can be found as well in certain poets, artists, philosophers, and those who serve the poor. And in broader and more pervasive ways, the healing wisdom that we are attempting to explore is found in the souls of men and women, too numerous to mention, who seek to live in obediential fidelity to the unseen light that sustains and guides them amid their own circumstances. And I should add, as well, that this timeless healing wisdom is present to some degree in you, as well, as evidenced by the very fact that you are drawn to read a book such as this.

The same light that shines out from the world's wisdom traditions also illumines the path that has led in this very moment to our encounter in these reflections. To clarify what I mean, I invite you to look back on your life, through all its twists and turns, and discern how it has come to pass that you have arrived at this point in which you are drawn to recognize and care about the subtle, interior dimensions of healing that we are exploring in these reflections. Seeing our life in this way allows us to appreciate how mysteriously we have been led, perhaps through many setbacks and confusing moments, along a providential path not of our own making.

To help you see your own life from this luminous perspective, I will lead the way by offering you in these reflections a kind of teaching memoir, in which I will trace out the lessons I have learned in my ongoing efforts to find my own way along the healing path. I will begin with my experiences of being repeatedly traumatized in my childhood and adolescence. I will share how my trauma was the opening through which God accessed me, sustaining me and letting me know I was not alone in the midst of my difficulties. I will share how these graced visitations in the midst of my ongoing trauma led me, upon graduating from high school, to enter the monastery, where I was radicalized and transformed forever in God's sustaining mercy.

I will share how the further trauma I experienced in the monastery sent me back out into the world, where I continued along a winding path that eventually prompted me to begin leading contemplative retreats. It was on that path that I met Maureen, and thereafter began our life together, which has led me up to this very moment. As I share my journey in this way, I will also be suggesting ways that you can look back at your life in this same reflective manner, noting the lessons of healing and transformation that you have learned along the way.

I can move in closer to the formative energies that led directly to the writing of this book by sharing with you a longstanding pattern that began to emerge in my life with Maureen. Every other Friday Maureen would drive me to the airport where I would fly out to lead a silent contemplative retreat, most often at a Catholic retreat house in the United States or Canada. I felt that those who came to these retreats, having read the description and knowing that the retreat would be conducted in silence, were drawn in part by this knowledge. Those who came knew that the meals would be eaten in silence and that everyone would be encouraged to maintain a spirit of silence throughout the weekend. They knew that there would be twenty-minute sessions of shared silent meditation and prayer before each conference. They also knew I would be sharing insights from the writings of Thomas Merton, Saint Teresa of Avila, or Meister Eckhart, as well as other mystics and spiritual teachers. All of these things had drawn their interest. But more succinctly still, I sensed that they were drawn to attend the retreats by unconsummated longing they did not understand for a union with God they did not understand, but which they knew was real and true because they had already been graced with moments in which they fleetingly tasted that union, present yet hidden in each passing moment of their lives.

Then, on Sunday at noon, I would leave the communal silence and serenity of the retreat to fly back to Los Angeles, where on Monday morning Maureen and I would go to our two-office suite, where we would sit with the men and women coming to us for psychotherapy. Many of those were trauma survivors who wanted their spirituality to be a resource in their therapy. When they came in to see us, they would not simply tell us about their trauma. They would show it to us, allowing us to see their trauma in their faces and in their eyes as they spoke. And we could feel in our own bodies the places in their bodies where trauma had staked its claim on their lives.

What most surprised me as I went back and forth between these opposite realms of trauma and transcendence was that many of those coming to the retreats and those coming for therapy were essentially the same people, and I was one of them! For I was a contemplative seeker going through my own therapy for the long-term, internalized effects of the trauma I had endured in my childhood and adolescence. And I was a traumatized person who tasted traces of deep healing and liberation welling up from my wounded preciousness in the presence of God.

A good number of the insights and suggested guidelines for healing offered in these reflections gravitate around the ways in which each of us is a unique edition of the universal story of being human. And among the themes or plotlines that run through our lives are the endlessly varied ways in which we seek to be healed from all that hinders us along the risky and transformative paths in which birth and death, sorrow and endless liberation, are ribboned throughout our days.

As I move toward bringing this introduction to a close, I encourage you to be patient with me. I am but a seventy-six-year-old man hoping to pass on a few things that might help you before I disappear. I encourage you as well to be patient with yourself. For patience ripens into humility, itself an opening to the healing path we are attempting to explore.

As a way to bring this introduction to a close, I share with you a story that I hope will help to orientate you to the intimate nature of the spiritual dimensions of healing that we are now beginning to explore. This story was told to me some years ago by Sister Mary Luke Tobin, who was mother superior of the Sisters of Loretto and a longtime friend of Thomas Merton. The story is taken from the tradition of the desert fathers and mothers. In the first centuries of the church these men and women went into the desert to undergo an interior martyrdom of dying to all that hindered them from experiencing the mystical dimensions of the promises of Christ. Men and women living in the surrounding villages would follow these solitary seekers into the desert and ask to receive from them a "word." By that, they meant a message, in the hearing of which, their hearts would be awakened to a deeper realization of God's presence in their lives.

In this story a Christian hermit heard a knock at the door of his hermitage. When he opened the door, he saw a mother and father and their young daughter. The parents apologized for intruding on the hermit's solitude but said they had come to ask him to pray over their daughter, whom ("as you can plainly see") an evil wizard had turned into a donkey.

"Yes, I see," said the hermit, as he invited them to come in. The hermit then asked the parents to sit off to one side as he asked the little girl if she was hungry and would like something to eat. When she said she would like that, the hermit talked to her as he prepared her a meal. Then, as she ate, he continued talking to her, asking her questions about things that mattered to her.

When the parents saw the love with which the hermit prepared their daughter some food and the sincere affection in which he spoke with her, their eyes were opened. They suddenly realized that the wizard had not cast a spell on their daughter, turning her into a donkey. Rather, the wizard had cast a spell on them, leading them to believe their daughter was a donkey. In seeing that their daughter was truly the little girl they loved, they were filled with joy and tearfully embraced her.

As the parents left with their daughter, they expressed their gratitude for what had just happened. And their daughter was grateful as well. For it is hard being a little girl when your parents think you are a donkey. It is especially hard when you fall into the shame-based suffering that comes when you start to believe that you are indeed the donkey your parents believe you to be. The deep healing that the little girl and her parents experienced in this story bears witness to the deep healing that I hope to explore in this book.

May your reading of these reflections in a sincere and heartfelt manner help you find your way yet further along the healing path on which you have already embarked. As you continue on this way, I hope that you will continue to discover, in all sorts of unexpected ways, that you are becoming a healing presence in an all-too-often traumatized and traumatizing world. By that, I mean you will continue to be graced with realizations that you are becoming someone in whose presence others are better able to experience the gift and miracle of who they really are deep down and who they are called to be, so that they in turn can pass on the contagious energy of healing to others.

Amen. So be it.

My Childhood Initiation into Trauma and Transcendence

It has been about a month since I wrote the Intro-duction, in which I shared with you the intimate exchanges between Maureen and myself as she was dying. She lived through that night. Then, without ever regaining consciousness, she died the next morning, ever so gently, slipping away like a whisper. Her ashes are next to me here as I write this now, in much the way that she would sit with me each morning as I wrote reflections such as these.

In the days and nights since her passing I have con-tinued to experience the same bittersweet alchemy that I shared with you in the Introduction. By that I mean that I continue to move back and forth between know-ing in my heart that I still love her as much as ever and knowing that she still loves me from within the depth of God's infinite love that is too overwhelmingly close and all-pervasive for me to understand and endure within the limits of my finite heart.

But most of the time such luminous consolations are not at all what I have been experiencing. For in the days and nights since her death I have been immersed in feelings of the unbearable pain of Maureen and me not being able to see and touch and be with each other in the simple rituals of love we knew so well. To be honest with you, in some very deep way I do not want to live any more on this earth without Maureen. If I could die tonight in my sleep, I would be immensely grateful. And so, I have been going back and forth about whether or not I have a right to write this book. For how can I, with integrity, hope to say anything here that might help you to experience the spiritual dimensions of healing that I feel so powerless to find? But in reflecting on the matter, I have had an insight that allows me to proceed with some degree of confidence. The insight being that this is not the first time I have felt so utterly lost and unhappy.

As you will soon see, the light of God's healing presence first flowed into me as a small child in the midst of overwhelming trauma. The healing light of God's presence that emerged out of that darkness continued to sustain me in the midst of ongoing trauma, leading me, upon graduation from high school, to enter the monastery. And it was there, in nearly six years of cloistered silence and prayer, that I was radicalized and transformed forever in God's sustaining mercy.

Then, just when I thought I was home free, I was further traumatized in the monastery. Everything fell apart in painful ways that led me out of the monastery back out into the world, where the darkness once again gave way to healing liberations that I would never have known had I not gone through the darkness. It was, in fact, years later, in the midst of a new period of darkness and struggle, that I first met Maureen, who came to an evening retreat in which I explored the teachings of Saint John of the Cross on the dark night of the soul. That encounter eventually led to the nearly thirty years of loving and being loved by each other in ways that deepened our shared experience of God's loving presence in our lives. And it was in the midst of that ongoing sweet communion that Maureen died, leaving me in my present state of painful darkness.

Seeing my life in this way, can I not hope and trust that this present darkness in which I feel so lost is simply the most recent crest of a wave in which God's sustaining presence has not yet broken through the sorrow in which I once again feel so lost? And is it not possible that writing this book with the sincere intention to help you experience the spiritual dimensions of healing in your life just might prove to be the opening through which the healing presence of God will once again make itself known in my life?

It is with sensitivities and intentions such as these that I am now sharing how I found my way to the healing path we are about to explore. Here is my first memory. Here is how my life as I remember it began.

I am standing near the window in the living room of the house on Bruner Street in Akron, Ohio. I am looking up at my father coming toward me, I think to pick me up and hold me. Instead, he seizes hold of me and throws me across the room. My face hits the leg of a table. I fall to the ground crying. The place where my face hit the table feels hot. My father walks toward me, stands over me for a moment, then walks away saying nothing. This is my first memory. This is how my life as I remember it began. I am three, maybe four years old.

The memory continues on with my mother and grandmother getting me ready that night to take me to the circus. They are putting talcum powder on my face to hide the bruise where my face hit the table. At the circus there is a lion in a red cage with large wheels trimmed in gold. My grandmother is holding me, saying something about how careful we need to be not to get too close to the cage. In my mind I am pairing up that lion with my father, wondering why my father is not in a cage.

This was the first memory from an ongoing pattern of my father's explosive, alcohol-fueled violence, directed repeatedly at my mother, my four younger brothers, and myself. The only one in the house who never had to worry about being hit by my father was my sister. It was not until years later that I was able to realize that she escaped this violence because he was sexually abusing her and thus claimed her as his own in ways that were as destructive and confusing as anything the rest of us in our fear of his rage and physical violence had to endure.

Once, when I was still quite young, my father told me that whenever his own father entered a room, he and his brothers had to jump out of their seats so their father could choose which chair he wanted to sit in. The one who got up last got a rap on the head with his knuckles as punishment for not rising fast enough. In that way, my father told me, their father made men out of him and his brothers. That, he told me, was what he was trying to do for me. My problem, he said, was that I was "angel sweet," and it was his job to beat that sweetness out of me. I can still remember trying to figure out what being "angel sweet" meant, thinking that if I could try not to be so angel sweet my father could love me instead of hurting me and scaring me all the time.

Sometimes my father's violence would come abruptly without warning, causing me to be hypervigilant, like an animal watching for predators that might attack at any moment. And sometimes my father's anger would mount slowly, as he became increasingly intoxicated, angry, and incoherent. I don't know which I dreaded more, the explosive violence that came without warning or those moments when his anger would become more and more intense, letting me know that at any moment I or someone in the room was going to be hit and that there was nothing any of us could do about it. The moment of actual violence brought a sense of relief in knowing that the terrible feeling of powerlessness in the face of impending violence was over. When I was taking a shower, I would sometimes hit myself in the face and on my chest and arms and legs as a way to take matters into my own hands by ritualistically reenacting the relief that came as soon as my father hit me or my mother or one of my brothers. I felt ashamed about this secret way of making myself feel better.

And yet it was during these ongoing childhood experiences of trauma that I first began to experience God's presence in my life through the formative influence of my mother, who was a devout Roman Catholic. Catholicism was one of the topics that would ignite my father's rage toward my mother. When my mother would take me and my younger siblings to mass on Sunday, she would tell us to pray to God to give us the strength to get through the scary things that happened when Daddy gets mad.

One night, when I was about four years old, I remember lying in bed in the dark, feeling very sad and afraid because I could hear my father yelling at my mother outside the door. I knew that at any moment he might hit her. I was feeling sad and afraid because earlier that day he had yelled at me and maybe had hit me. I felt sad and afraid because I knew that the next day, if he wanted to, he would hit me again and there was nothing that anyone could do to stop him.

Lying there in the dark, listening to my father raging at my mother, I took what my mother taught me to heart. I prayed the way frightened children pray, asking God to help me endure the ongoing terror and sadness that permeated my life in those days. In a moment I cannot remember, God heard my prayer, came to me in the dark, and took me to a secret place in God where the violence couldn't find me.

The next day and in the days that followed, the violence continued, but things were actually better. Now, when my father got angry and hit me, he didn't know that he was only hitting that other little boy, that effigy of myself that others could see. He did not know the more real me, who was safely hidden away in the secret place in God that my father knew nothing about. When I was at mass on Sundays with my mother and younger siblings, I can recall looking up into the stained-glass windows of the church with the images of Jesus, the angels, and the saints. Just as I had paired up my father with the lion in the cage, I paired up the inside of the church with the secret place inside of God where the violence could not find me.

When I was seven years old, I made my first holy communion. With childlike, devotional sincerity I believed that Jesus was truly present in the concentrated host. On Sundays at mass, after going up to receive communion, I would return to my place beside my mother, There, I would kneel, close my eyes, place my face in my hands, and hold very still. Kneeling there inside the church, I sensed that I was kneeling inside of God, who, in the consecrated host I had just received, was also inside of me. Kneeling there inside of God-inside-of-me deeply affected me in intimate and consoling ways that I could not and did not need to understand. Yet I sensed, in these moments of silent stillness, that I was granted my first taste of what it must be like to be in heaven.

It was then, in the midst of these experiences, that I was initiated into the mysterious ways in which the polar opposite realms of trauma and transcendence meet and merge to form a bittersweet alchemy. It was then that the peace of God that surpasses all understanding began to emerge and sustain me in my life.

As a way to end this first chapter, I will share an insight that came to me in reflecting on being with Maureen as she breathed her last breath. We begin our life on this earth by taking in our first breath, which allows us to cry out, announcing our presence in the world. Throughout the course of our lives we continuously inhale and exhale, inhale and exhale, in our passage through time from birth to death. When the moment of death finally comes our last act on this earth is to exhale. This is what happened as I sat next to Maureen with my hand on her shoulder. Her breathing became irregular. She would exhale. Then there would be a pause in which she would suddenly inhale. Until finally, she exhaled but did not inhale, leading me to realize that the moment of death itself is not an event but a cessation, a ceasing of the next life-sustaining inhalation.

From the vantage point of our ego consciousness this is true. But when understood from the spiritual point of view that we will explore in these reflections, another more expansive, poetic way of understanding can emerge. We begin to realize that when we are born and take in our first breath, God is exhaling himself, whole and complete in and as the gift and miracle of our very life. We move on in our passage through time, sustained by God, inhaling/exhaling, inhaling/exhaling through all our days. Then, when the moment of death finally arrives, we exhale and do not inhale. And in our final exhalation God inhales us back into the infinite depth of God, which is our true and eternal home.

Thus, God interiorly spoke to the thirteenth-century Christian mystic Mechtild of Magdeburg, telling her not to fear her death. God told her, "For in that moment I will breathe in my breath, and your soul will come to me like a needle to a magnet."[1]

May each of us learn to discern in the life-sustaining rhythm of our breath traces of the deathless presence of God, which sustains us and ever will sustain us up to and including the moment of our death and beyond. Amen. So be it.

---

[1] Mechtild of Magdeburg, *The Flowing Light of the Godhead*, trans. Frank Tobin and Margot Schmidt (New York: Paulist Press, 1998), 214.

2

Strangely Tattered,
Strangely Whole

When I was twelve years old, my mother told me that at night when my younger siblings and I were asleep, my father would hit her and become so violently angry that she was afraid he might kill her. She said that because I was the oldest, she was asking me to stay awake at night, to sit at the top of the stairs and listen. If I thought he was starting to kill her, I was to run down the stairs and out into street to pound on a neighbor's door so they could call the police.

If my father was in a good mood when I went upstairs to bed, I felt it was safe for me to go to sleep. But quite often he would already be in an angry mood when I and my younger siblings went to bed. And so I would keep my vigil, sitting at the top of stairs, listening, trying to figure out if he was just hitting her again, grabbing hold of her, pulling her hair, or if was he starting to kill her. And I would feel the weight of not knowing what to do. What if I ran down the stairs and he beat me to the front door—would he kill me? What if his rage escalated to the point that he was about to kill her, and I did not run out to get help soon enough—would I be responsible for my mother's death?

My mother telling me she was afraid that my father might kill her deepened my trauma in a more interior way as I became consciously aware of my own fears that my father might kill me. I did not think that he would intentionally kill me in a premeditative way. Rather, I sensed that when he was drunk his rage toward me would at times become so intense that he might kill me without consciously intending to do so.

It was in these ongoing traumatizing conditions that I learned to survive by being hypervigilant, looking for the first signs that my father was beginning to become angry at my mother, my younger brothers, or me. I learned to survive by being as passive as I could, doing my best to do whatever my father wanted me to do, so as not to trigger his rage. I learned to survive by living in a habitual dissociative state that allowed me interiorly to distance myself from feelings of intense fear that were too overwhelming for me to bear. And most of all, I learned to survive by being as interiorly grounded as I could be in God's sustaining presence, which protected me from nothing, even as it inexplicably sustained me in the ongoing, atmospheric traumas that pervaded my life in those days.

It was in this pervasive ongoing trauma that a heightened sense of God's presence flowed into my life in a book titled *Our Lady of Fatima* by William Thomas Walsh. It was given to me by my mother's sister, my aunt Lucile, who was a nun who lived in Cleveland, about an hour and half drive from where we lived in Akron.

The book told the story of Mary, the mother of Jesus, appearing to three children in Fatima, Portugal, in 1918. As word got out that these visions were occurring, large numbers of people began gathering to be in the presence of the children as they went into an ecstatic state of deep prayer in Mary's presence.

As time went on, a church was built on the site where these apparitions occurred. As with the shrine in Lourdes, France, honoring the apparitions of Mary to Saint Bernadette, these sites became and remain to this day places of pilgrimage where people come to pray. In both sites there are alcoves lined with crutches and wheelchairs and other mementos of miraculous cures that are granted on these pilgrimages.

At twelve years old I was deeply affected by the Fatima story. What most got to me in a singular way was that the children said the presence of God, which came over them in the presence of the angel, was so compelling that when each angelic visitation ended they found it difficult to move for some time afterward. This helped me realize that I might learn from God to experience God's presence in the interior dimensions of my traumatized body.

Moved by the presence of God that came over me in reading this story, I nailed a holy water font just inside the entrance to my bedroom so I could dip my fingers in holy water and bless myself each time I entered and left my bedroom. I made an altar on a small table on which I placed a statue of Mary, my Bible, holy cards with images of Jesus and the saints, and a candle in a small container made of blue glass.

Each night after supper as it was getting dark and my mother and father and younger siblings were still downstairs watching television on our small black and white television set, I would go up to my room. I would close the door, bless myself with holy water, turn out the light, light the candle, and kneel on the floor. As my eyes adjusted to the delicate blue light that illumined the statue of Mary, the images of Jesus and saints, and the walls of my room, I would pray the rosary as my way to open myself to God's presence in my life. At the end of each decade of ten Hail Marys, I would bow over and touch my forehead to the floor the way devout Muslims do when they pray. And bowing there in the dark I would whisper the prayer that the angel taught the children to pray: "My God, I believe, I adore, I hope, and I love you. I ask pardon for those who do not believe in you, who do not hope, who do not love you." As I ended my rendezvous with God in prayer, I would blow out the candle, turn on the light, and go down to join my family watching television. Later on, when the six of us children would come up to bed, I would keep my vigil at the top of the stairs, listening to my father raging at my mother.

As I look back at these experiences now, what most stands out to me is a truth of the awakening heart known to those who have been fortunate enough to have experienced it. This truth being the surprising re-alization that from the hidden depths of a darkness too terrible to name or explain, God can emerge as a sovereign, silent presence that carries us forward, amazed and grateful, into realms of clarity and fulfillment that we could scarcely have imagined.

Please notice that I have been sharing my story from the vantage point of my experience of myself as a traumatized child illumined by intimate realizations of God's presence, sustaining me and letting me know that I was not alone in the midst of my difficulties. At this point I am inviting you join me in moving yet further along the healing path by reflecting with me on a playful parable, a kind of waking dream.

Jesus often taught in parables, meaning stories that embody and bear witness to how God is present in the foundational experiences of our lives. As our eyes adjust to the divine light shining out from the parable, we can begin to join God in seeing how God sees and is present in the intimate, interior dimensions of the situation in which we find ourselves.

In this spirit I invite you to imagine that you are sitting alone in the middle of a well-lit room. There are no windows and no furniture in the room other than the chair you are sitting in. The ceiling, floor, and four bare walls of the room are all white. As you sit there alone in silence, the light in the room slowly begins to dim. As the room dims, a light on the other side of the wall you are facing slowly becomes brighter and brighter. You begin to realize that the wall you are facing is not really a solid wall, as you had imagined, but is rather a gossamer veil that is becoming increasingly translucent in the light that is shining through it, filling the darkness of your room with an unfamiliar light.

In the light shining out from the other side of the veil you see God, the angels, and the saints. They are all laughing and waving at you, letting you know how delighted they are that you can see them. You start laughing and waving back at them.

Then God, the angels, and the saints pass through the veil to join you, rendering the room radiant with communal joy and delight in which your very presence begins to glow with the presence of God. Illumined and transformed in this way, God and the angels and saints carry you with them into heaven, just on the other side of the veil, where all are dwelling who have died and crossed over into God. Then God and the angels and saints carry you with them back through the veil, back to the room, now aglow with heavenly wonder and delight. Then, once again, they transport you back into the celestial realm, and then back again into the room, then back again through the veil into paradise, then back again through veil into the room.

As the ecstatic, dreamlike wonder of this graced moment of awakening begins to dissipate as mysteriously as it began, you are left once again in the familiarity of your earthly experience of yourself sitting there alone in the room, facing the wall. But while everything is the same as before, everything is, in an interior way, radically different. For you now realize that while, yes, it is true that, on one level, the wall you are facing really is a wall, understood as the point beyond which your finite eyes cannot see and through which your physical body cannot pass, yet in the afterglow of the unitive experience that has just graced your life, you now know in the depths of your awakened heart that, ultimately speaking, the wall is no wall at all. You know that, yes, there is a veil through which God's oneness with us is interiorly known to us "as in a mirror darkly" (1 Cor 13:12). Yet, in the more interior dimensions of your awakening heart, you know that, ultimately speaking, there is no veil at all, except the one that exists in your finite, yet-to-be-fully-awakened mind. For you have been graced with a fleeting experience of being immersed in God-immersed-in-you in a boundless communion that utterly transcends, even as it utterly permeates, the darkness and fragmentations of this world.

I am now inviting you to join me as I allow the light shining out from this parable to illumine more interior aspects of my experience of moving back and forth between praying alone in my room and sitting at the top of the stairs, filled with fear, listening to my father raging at my mother. My hope is that my sharing how I have learned to see my life in the light of this parable will help you to see your own life in this same light, thus allowing you to enter more deeply into God's oneness with you in the circumstances in which you find yourself.

Returning to my story, now illumined by the parable, I recall how I would go to my room in the evening to pray. As I knelt on the floor with my rosary wrapped around my hands, the darkness in which I was kneeling was, at the surface level, merely the darkness of the room illumined by the blue light of the vigil candle shining through its glass container. At a more interior level, illumined by the parable, the darkness in which I knelt in prayer was inside of me as a traumatized twelve-year-old boy, kneeling there in the outer darkness, all the while feeling like a ghost made of fear and sadness and the dissociative confusion that spared me from having to experience overwhelming feelings too bewildering and scary to endure. And, at an infinitely deeper, more interior level, the darkness in which I knelt in prayer was the primordial darkness in which God's hidden presence was sustaining me in ways I could not and did not need to comprehend.

When I lit the vigil candle in the little blue glass container, the delicate light that illumined the four walls of my room was simply the light coming from the small flame of the candle. At a more interior level, illumined by the parable, the light of that little candle was the light of God's presence that was not simply illuminating the walls of my room but was the unseen light of God in which I knelt in prayer.

At one level, as I bowed over in devotional sincerity, touching my forehead to the floor, I was simply a devout, traumatized, twelve-year-old boy praying for dear life, asking God to sustain me and guide me in the midst of an ongoing nightmare in sensing that I might not survive. At a more interior level, illumined by the parable, as I bowed over in the dark, my very presence glowed with the presence of God, giving itself to me whole and complete in and as the gift and miracle of my very presence, so strangely tattered, yet so strangely whole in the midst of my fear and confusion.

When my prayerful vigil with God ended, I would blow out the candle, bless myself with holy water, leave my room and then, as my younger brothers and my sister slept, I would sit at the top of the stairs keeping my other vigil, listening to my father as he raged incoherently at my mother. And as I sat at the top of the stairs, the intensity in my father's voice flooded me once again with renewed waves of fear that closed off any sense of access to the delicate illuminations that just moments before had so blessed and sustained me in prayer.

As this pattern was repeated over and over again in the weeks and months of moving back and forth between the polar opposite realms of prayerful vigil in God and being flooded with feelings of traumatizing terror during my watchful vigil at the top of the stairs, a new awareness too deep to feel and understand slowly emerged within me. For in looking back at these moments, I can see how I was being led by God into enigmatic and paradoxical waters in which I was invited to realize that ultimately speaking there is no wall, no barrier between the polar opposite realms of trauma and transcendence that meet and merge and interpenetrate each other in endlessly varied ways throughout our lives.

Even now, as I write this, I am still learning to settle into these paradoxical waters in an ongoing and substantial way. For me, currently, this means learning to accept and trust that Maureen's deathless presence flows unseen and unfelt in the pervasive sense of sadness and loss in which I am sitting here beside her ashes. I sit here knowing and trusting that if I do not panic and run off here and there to avoid the feelings of pain and loss, I will continue to sense in the depths of my loss her deathless presence, inseparably entwined with the deathless presence of God, bringing me face to face with the deep healing that spirituality has and will continue to bring into my life.

When I left the monastery and began to lead silent contemplative retreats and be with the men and women coming to me for psychotherapy, people shared with me their own childhood experiences of God's presence in their lives. I will now share with you two of these stories of childhood encounters with God. The first encounter bears witness to the ways the light of the parable shines so unexpectedly in the happy moments of our lives as children. The second encounter embodies the way the light of the parable shines into sad and scary moments of our lives as children. Both stories together embody how these initial awakenings, so marked and limited as they are by immature and perhaps even infantile distortions, nonetheless contain undercurrents of divinity that can emerge in clearer, more reality-based ways throughout our lives.

The first encounter occurred on a weekend contemplative retreat in which an elderly woman came to me saying that in the communal silence of the retreat she found herself recalling how as a young girl living on the family farm she would go out alone in the summer into the apple orchard. She would lie down alone in the tall grass of the orchard, holding very still, watching the clouds go by overhead. She looked at me and said with a note of clarity in her voice, "Something was given to me there." By the look in her eye as she spoke, I sensed that what was given to her in the orchard so many years ago was as fresh and real to her as the moment in which she was sharing with me this graced awakening. I sensed too that, in entrusting me with this story, she was hoping, trusting, that she would not be standing there alone, unseen and unmet in her self-disclosures, but would rather be standing with me as someone who could see with her the timeless gift granted to her in this graced childhood memory.

The second encounter occurred with a woman who was coming to me in my psychotherapy practice, seeking help for pervasive feelings of sadness and loneliness. When I asked her how far back we would have to go to the first time she could remember having these feelings, she traced these feeling back to how afraid she would feel as a young girl when her parents would frequently argue in front of her. What she singled out as the most painful aspect of these memories is how completely unaware her parents were of how their rage toward each other flooded her with feelings of overwhelming fear and sadness.

She remembered how, one summer night, as her parents were in the midst of one their intense arguments, she opened the patio screen door and went out, unnoticed, into the backyard. She climbed up into the low branches of a tree. And as she sat there alone in the dark in the low branches of that tree, she closed one eye and lined up a twig with a star. She recalled saying to God, "If you know I am here, make that star move to the other side of that twig." She recalled thinking that if the star moved, it would be a kind of secret between her and God. She told me that God did not move the star. And then she said, almost as an afterthought, "But there is something about the remembrance of myself sitting alone in the dark in the low branches of that tree waiting for God to move a star that consoles me."

I recall telling her that I could not help noticing that, yes, it was true that God did not move the star, but what was so striking is that all these years later she was moved in some interior way in remembering that moment and that I was moved as she entrusted me with this memory.

A poetic understanding of her therapy emerged from this moment—that whenever she felt stuck in her therapy, whenever we did not know just how to go on, we could think of ourselves as sitting together in the low branches of that tree, waiting for God to move that star. And in this way the closed horizon of her traumatized self might become once again more translucent to the graced and guiding light in which her healing might continue to deepen and unfold.

When the spiritual awakenings of children are actually occurring, they are momentarily held in a timeless moment of awe in which their newly emerging experience of themselves in ego consciousness is transcended and held, in ever so delicate ways, in the light of God. Children who are blessed in this way will sometimes try to tell their parents about these awakenings by saying things that are beyond their years. But most often children blessed in this way tend not speak of these experiences because they cannot begin to find words that would allow them to share such things. The awakenings remain within them as wondrous secrets that often fade from their awareness as they face the complexities and challenges that come with the passage of time. But with some children these flashes of divinity soak into the hidden recesses of their body and into the hidden depths of their soul, where they continue to stir now and again with renewed and deepened clarity beyond what a child, or even we as adults, can understand.

My intuitive understanding of such things is that when poets and artists and all those whose lives have been radicalized along a creative trajectory trace out the origins of their creative journey, they often find themselves looking back to moments in their childhood when these graced inclinations first began to appear in their lives. This, of course, is not always the case. For the spirit is like the wind that blows where it pleases, and so quite often the awakenings do not appear until much later in life, perhaps not until we are dying. Perhaps such graced awakenings do not occur at all in vivid and defining ways until we pass through the veil of death into God, who fulfills and resolves these things in ways that are beyond what our finite minds can comprehend.

In attempting to understand the spiritual awakenings of children, it is helpful to realize that the first flash of divinity, granted to them in such moments, transcends and illumines their newly emerging experience of themselves in ego consciousness. As the unseen light of these fleeting awakenings dissipates, the child's experience of itself in ego consciousness glows for a moment with lingering traces of the divine light that children are, from time to time, so privileged to experience. The initial flash of awakening is infinite. The afterglow of that light lingering on in the child's memory is finite.

A child's understanding of its self-transcending awakenings unfolds within the child according to the limits and distortions of a child's understanding. A traumatized child's understanding of its self-transcending awakenings unfolds within the limits and distortions of a traumatized child's understanding.

It seems to me that this transformative process continues on throughout our lives. For as long as we are on this earth, we are children of the light finding our way through darkness. The task, it seems to me, is for us to continue to pass beyond immature understanding of spiritual matters formed in times of innocence and in times of trauma and abandonment by learning to cultivate more mature, reality-based ways of understanding the deep healing that spirituality brings into our lives. At the same time, we must be careful not to allow our adult, conceptual comprehension of such things to close off the childlike opening of wonder through which the graces and gifts of God flow into our lives. We must always keep in mind, as Gabriel Marcel phrased it, that "we do not see the light; rather, we are the aperture through which it shines."

May each of us, in our own unique way, experience the healing energies that flow into our lives as we learn to join God in knowing who God knows and calls us to be. And may our lifelong fidelity to this learning curve of amazement and gratitude, though it be mingled with fear and sorrow, spill over into the ways we see and treat the people we meet and live with each day.

Amen. So be it.

3

The Sign of Jonas

When I was in the eighth grade my devotional sincerity led me to feel and believe that God was calling me to be a priest. This was in 1956, before the Second Vatican Council. The Mass was still celebrated in Latin, and so, in looking ahead to going into the ninth grade, I wanted to leave the public school system to attend Archbishop Hoban High School, the all-boys Catholic high school in Akron, where I could study Latin in preparation for going to the seminary after graduation.

I knew my parents could not afford the tuition at the Catholic high school, so I walked to our parish church, rang the doorbell, and asked to speak to one of the priests. Father Thomas Rath heard my story about needing financial aid so that I could go to the Catholic high school in preparation for the priesthood. He arranged for the parish to pay for my tuition for my four years at Hoban and to pay me twenty-five cents an hour in exchange for working three days a week after school from 4 pm to 9 pm at the rectory, answering the door and the telephone. The hours I spent three nights a week in the parish rectory provided a haven of safety and peace away from the chaos of my life at home. When I walked home at night from my job at the parish, I would stop at my grandmother's house on Bruner Street. We would drink Constant Comment tea, laugh, and tell dirty jokes as we each smoked one of her hand-rolled cigarettes. She was, in a way, the matriarch on my mother's side of the family, strong in her faith, and offering me the love and attention I so badly needed.

The transition from public school to an all-boys Catholic school was very stressful. I felt embarrassed about my family being poor at a school where most of the other students seemed to me to be rich kids whose parents would drop them at school in big expensive cars. The hardest thing of all was that I felt completely lost in my Latin, algebra, and other courses. In the first grading period I failed Latin and algebra and barely got by in my other classes. I was taken out of Latin and algebra and other college preparatory classes and put into remedial English and math and other less demanding classes. Yet still I struggled, barely getting by.

I wish I could say that I believed I was having such a difficult time in my studies because my father had destroyed my mind. For that, at least, would have meant that I was consciously aware of the destructive effects the ongoing trauma was having on my ability to concentrate. But my understanding at the time was that I did not believe I had a mind. By that I mean that I did not think I had whatever it is that allowed the other students not only to pass Latin and algebra but to get "A's" in those courses. I felt ashamed about not having a mind. As I expressed it to myself at the time, I was ashamed of being dumb in a school where so many students were so smart.

But worst of all, for me, my inability to learn Latin meant I was not smart enough to be a priest. And so I found solace in knowing I could still commit myself to God by taking vows of poverty, chastity, and obedience as a lay brother in a religious community such as the Franciscans or the Congregation of Holy Cross who taught at the University of Notre Dame and the high school I was attending. I knew I was not smart enough to teach academic classes, but I could dedicate my life to God in the community and serve as a groundskeeper or cook or some other form of service that did not require academic abilities that I did not possess.

I was inspired by stories my grandmother told me of growing up in French-speaking Montreal, Canada, where a lay brother in the Congregation of Holy Cross named Brother André Bessette was known to be a holy man who served as porter, answering the door at the church. After taking care of each person who came to the door, he would return to the church, where he would spend long hours in silent prayer. In that humble service as porter mingled with long hours of silent prayer he crossed over into God. People who came to him asking for prayers began to experience miraculous cures. But although I was inspired by this story, I still had no clear sense of the path I was being called to follow.

Then, toward the end of my freshman year, the instructor in my religion class told us about monasteries. I had never heard of monasteries before. He described monasteries as places where people go to give themselves to God in a hidden life of poverty and prayer that channels God's grace into the world in ways we do not understand. He told us about Thomas Merton, who, as a young man studying at Columbia University, had a series of spiritual experiences that led him to be baptized in the Catholic Church and to enter the cloistered Trappist monastery of the Abbey of Gethsemani in Kentucky. In the monastery he wrote his spiritual autobiography, *The Seven Storey Mountain*, which made it onto the bestseller list of the *New York Times*. The teacher told us that Thomas Merton was still living in the monastery and writing books on spirituality that helped many people experience and respond to God's presence in their lives.

That day, after school, I went to the school library, where I found a book by Thomas Merton titled *The Sign of Jonas*, a journal he kept as a monk in the monastery. I read the second entry of that journal, dated December 13, 1946, in which Merton reveals something very intimate and mysterious about himself, writing, "I have only one desire and that is the desire for solitude—to disappear into God, to be submerged in His peace, to be lost in the secret of His face." Standing there, at fourteen years old, I did not fully understand what that meant. But something in me did. For, from somewhere deep within myself, I heard myself say, "Me too." Merton's words, welling up from the depths of his own awakened heart, accessed that same hidden depth in me, occasioning a radicalized understanding of myself as someone who longed for solitary communion with God. Such, it seems to me, are the mysterious interior conduits of grace in which transmissions of holiness and destiny flow from one awakening heart to another.

I knew at that moment that I did not want to stop reading Thomas Merton, whose words spoke to me so deeply of my own desire for God. And so I checked *The Sign of Jonas* out of the library and soon after bought my own copy. As I read Merton alone in my room, it became clear to me that Merton had found his way into the secret of God's face. A master plan emerged within me. I would trust that God would help me survive the remaining three years of high school. Then, when I graduated from high school, I would enter the monastery, where I would sit at Merton's feet so he could guide me into the secret of God's face. I began to write to the monk who was the vocation director at the monastery, telling him of my desire to enter the monastery when I graduated. I gave him my grandmother's address so my father would not see the mail coming from the monastery.

As you reflect on all that I have shared about how traumatized I was in feeling lost and broken in so many ways it might seem puzzling that I would be so bold as to write to the monastery. Know that it never would have occurred to me to be so bold had Merton in his writings spoken of himself as a realized spiritual master who had found his way into spiritual heights that were beyond anything that anyone such as myself could ever hope to achieve. Instead, he spoke of himself as someone who was so deeply aware of and accepting of his own poverty and limitations in the presence of God that he helped me to recognize God's presence within myself in the midst of my own poverty and limitations. What is more, he helped me to realize that my humble acceptance of my poverty and limitations in the presence of God was the condition in which the union with God I longed for would continue to deepen and unfold within me in unforeseeable ways.

The next three years continued as before with my ongoing faith in God sustaining me in the midst of my ongoing trauma. During those three years my father knew nothing about my plans to enter the monastery. A few days after I graduated from high school, I saw him trimming the hedges along the front of the yard and decided this was as good a moment as any. After telling him about my desire to enter the monastery, he wanted to know what a monastery was, since he had never heard of such a thing. With my voice shaking with fear, I did my best to explain to him that I felt God was calling me to go the monastery as a place where I could give myself to God in silence and prayer.

As I spoke, I could see his jaw tighten, which was one of the warning signs that he was getting angry. Then he said in a quiet, determined voice, "If you go to that place, I will kill your mother to punish you!" I remember him saying, "That's not a threat. It's a promise. I will kill her if you go to that place!" I walked away in silence, knowing within myself that I had a right to save my life. I had a right to do what I believed in my heart God was calling me to do.

I got up very early the next morning when it was still dark. I left a note on my bed saying that I was going to the monastery. I walked as quietly as I could out of my bedroom into the darkened hallway and down the stairs. Our dog came up to me wagging her tail, as if to wonder why I was up in the middle of the night. I left the house and walked in a light rain to Saint Bernard Church, where I attended the 6:00 a.m. Mass. During the Mass I kept looking over my shoulder for fear my father might come bursting into the church to do some terrible thing to me. When the Mass ended, I walked across the street to the Greyhound bus station to board the bus that would take me to the monastery.

The following passage in the writings of Thomas Merton seems to be fitting way to conclude this chapter. As we read this passage in a prayerful and careful manner, may we discern within ourselves traces of the deepening trust in God of which he speaks.

My Lord God, I have no idea where I am going. I do not see the road ahead of me. I cannot know for certain where it will end. Nor do I really know myself, and the fact that I think that I am following your will does not mean that I am actually doing so. But I believe that the desire to please you does in fact please you. And I hope I have that desire in all that I am doing. I hope that I will never do anything apart from that desire. And I know that if I do this you will lead me by the right road, though I may know nothing about it. Therefore will I trust you always, though I may seem to be lost and in the shadow of death. I will not fear, for you are ever with me, and you will never leave me to face my perils alone.[1]

Amen. So be it.

[1]Thomas Merton, *Thoughts in Solitude* (New York: Farrar, Straus & Giroux, 1956, 1958), 83.

4

Entering the Monastery

When I arrived at the monastery, I went through the door in the guesthouse that led up into the balcony of the vast interior of the monastic church. I have long since forgotten what I said to God as I knelt and then sat there in silence. But I keenly remember the realizations that washed over me in those moments as I sensed God speaking within me, without words, asking: Can you not see how strange and wonderful it is that I heard you praying to me in the dark as a frightened three-year-old child? Can you not see how strange and wonderful it is that I accessed you as I did, in such secret and intimate ways, letting you know you were not alone in the midst of the sad and scary things that were happening to you in those days? Can you not see how strange and wonderful it is that I let you know in that ninth-grade religion class that there are places called monasteries where I draw people to seek and to find and to give themselves to me in silence and prayer? And how I prompted you to listen closely as the teacher spoke of Thomas Merton, who lives as a monk in this very monastery in which you are now sitting in my presence? And can you not see how strange and wonderful it is that I prompted you to go to the school library to pull from the shelf the journal that Thomas Merton wrote in this place? And how I was waiting for you to read Merton's desire to disappear into the secret of my face so that I, in that very moment, could awaken that same desire in you that I knew would lead you to this very place in which the desire to disappear into the secret of my face might be consummated?

Within the first few days of arriving at the guest-house I was interviewed by Father John of the Cross, the vocation director with whom I had been corresponding during my four years of high school. I was also interviewed by Father John Eudes, a member of the community who was a psychiatrist.

Father John Eudes asked me if I had any difficulties with depression, anxiety, or other psychological issues that might indicate that I was not called to the interior discipline and silence of the monastic life. I assured him that I had no such difficulties. In one sense I lied in telling him this because I was afraid that if I told him about the trauma and the ways it had affected me, he would not give permission for me to enter the monastery. And I felt so strongly that God was calling me to the monastic life that I felt I had a right to at least try it. At a more interior level I answered this way because I had been so deeply traumatized since I was a small child that I did not know I was traumatized. My fear-based traumatized self was my normal self.

My final interview was with the abbot. In meeting the abbot I was told that when I entered his office, I was to bow to him and kneel on the floor at his desk. As I knelt on the floor, I remember him telling me that Jesus was drawing me into the cloistered silence of the monastery so that he could lock the door and have me all to himself in a life of perpetual silence and prayer. And that my fidelity to this secret, intimate communion between myself and Jesus would touch and heal the world in mysterious and hidden ways.

After a few days one of the monks came to the guesthouse to lead me into the monastic enclosure in which I hoped I would be spending the rest of my life. As I was led from the guesthouse into the monastic enclosure, I looked up to see the words "God alone" inscribed in stone at the entrance of the monastery. From the depths of my interiorly awakened self I sensed something of the depth and beauty those words embodied and their meaning for the life I was about to enter.

Before I take you with me into the monastery I should clarify that I entered in July 1961, just as preparations for the Second Vatican Council were under way to bring about a spirit of renewal in the Catholic Church. For most Catholics in the world the most noticeable effects of this renewal would be that the Mass, which for centuries had been celebrated in Latin, would now be said in the language of the people in each country. This same spirit of renewal would also carry over into religious orders such as the Franciscans, the Jesuits, and the Cistercian monastic order that I had entered. I say this because some of the details of my daily life in the monastery were soon about to change. It is beyond the scope of these reflections as a memoir to go into the changes that occurred. But an insight by Thomas Merton conveys the spirit in which changes were made. Merton noted that all renewal in religious communities is an attempt to return to the original fire of the community's founder. In the case of the monastic life that fire was embodied in a Rule for monks written by Saint Benedict in the fifth century. In that Rule, he laid out details of a daily life of prayer, silence, humility, and simplicity in which the monk is to prefer nothing to Christ, in whom the monk seeks to be transformed in the deifying light of God.

Here then are some of the details of my new way of life in the monastery and the ways in which I experienced and understood each of these details as the devout, traumatized, just-out-of-high-school, would-be mystic with acne that I was in those days.

I slept each night on a straw mattress on boards in a small partitioned-off cubicle in a common dormitory. On the gray walls of each partitioned-off cell there were a few hooks for hanging clothes, a crucifix, and just inside the curtained-off entrance, a holy water font. In my devotional sincerity I found meaning in this, knowing that when Jesus was born in the stable in Bethlehem, he was laid in a straw-covered manger. I also felt solace in knowing that down through the ages, straw has been the bedding of the poor.

My hair was shaved off to symbolize my renunciation of the world's vanity. My clothes were exchanged for the brown habit of a lay brother postulant, letting me know that the clothes I now wore were the same as those worn by monks down through the ages to sacramentalize our desire to be clothed in the sustaining presence of God.

When someone first entered the monastery, the abbot chose the saint's name by which they would be known in the community. Often, the abbot would choose a name in accordance with the ethnic background of the new member. Because of my Irish background, I was given the name Brother Finbar. I looked up my namesake and discovered that Saint Finbar lived in the sixth century in County Cork, Ireland, first as a hermit and later as bishop. In this way I knew that my name grounded me in an ancient lineage of spiritually awakened seekers who would guide and help me in my own ongoing spiritual quest.

Actually, my name was Brother *Mary* Finbar, in that all the monks in the Cistercian Order I had entered took the name of Mary, the mother of Jesus and the archetype of the contemplative soul. In responding to the message of the angel that she was to be the mother of Jesus, Mary accepted the angel's message in praise of God, saying, "He has looked on his servant in her nothingness. Henceforth all generations will call me blessed" (Luke 1:46–55). In this way she exemplified my desire to experience the fullness of God's presence, filling my entire being in my nothingness without God.

Each day began at 2:30 in the morning with the waking bell, letting me know I had fifteen minutes to go upstairs to the lay brother novices' chapel to chant the Psalms of Vigils. We followed the ancient practice of keeping vigil, praying for the world as the world slept. For me, I also experienced Vigils as honoring Jesus, who, in the Garden of Gethsemane, on the night of his arrest by the Roman soldiers, came to the disciples who had fallen asleep, asking, "Can you not pray one hour with me?" (Mt 26:40).

The chanting of the Psalms in the wee hours of the night began my daily life of *ora et labora* (prayer and work) prescribed by Saint Benedict in his Rule. The paced rhythm of the day consisted of daily Mass, gathering for the seven canonical hours to chant the Psalms, and the daily labor needed to maintain and support the monastery, mingled with periods set aside for the prayerful reading of scripture and other spiritual works and quiet times to give ourselves over to seeking God in silent prayer and meditation.

We observed a vegetarian diet with a simple breakfast of bread and coffee. The noon meal consisted of soup made with yesterday's left-over vegetables, along with two other vegetables and bread. As we ate in silence, we listened to one of the monks who read to us from a spiritual book. After Vespers, we ate another simple meal, followed by time for reading and prayer.

Each day ended with chanting the Psalms of Compline and going to my cell at 7:30 pm to lie down on my straw mattress and drift off to sleep in my ongoing search for God.

Please notice that the tonal quality of devotional sincerity in my new life in the monastery was continuous with the tonal quality of the devotional sincerity of my high school years in which I knelt on the floor of my bedroom in the light that shined out from the blue glass vigil light and in which I was sustained in a primordial and hidden way in God's sustaining presence in my life.

As will become clear in the chapters yet to come, I had a long way to go in moving into more mature, reality-based ways of following the healing path we are exploring together in these reflections. I had longer still to learn how important it is not to fall prey to pseudo-sophisticated mannerisms of the mind and heart that close off the essentially childlike purity of contemplative intimacy with God.

May each of us continue to find our way along the healing path as we learn to discern and to outgrow childish and hurtful attitudes and ways of treating ourselves and others. And may we do so in such a way that we become ever more childlike in learning to see and delight in the incomprehensible stature of simple things—the beloved's smile, a slant of light across the floor, the smell of cinnamon, the palms of our own hands.

Amen. So be it.

5

Silence

In these reflections we are learning to discern the ways that God waits, hidden away, searching for openings through which to emerge in joyful moments, granting fleeting tastes of the high, high joy of God that utterly transcends, even as it utterly permeates, the joyful moments of our lives.

We are also seeking here to discern the ways God waits, hidden away, searching for openings through which to emerge in moments of sorrow, inspiring and empowering us to heal as best we can from all that hinders us from experiencing the peace of God that guides and sustains us in the midst of all that remains unresolved in our minds and hearts.

Some of these graced awakenings arise in the midst of the circumstances in which we find ourselves, inspiring us to be more loving, more patient, more courageous, more of whatever it is that adds to the richness and quality of our lives. And some of these graced awakenings are experienced as an interior call to commit ourselves to a whole new phase of our life—to get married, to start a family, to commit ourselves to cultivating a creative gift, or to devote ourselves to some form of service to the community, or, as in my case, to feel called by God to enter the monastery.

I went to the monastery assuming and hoping that as a novice newly entering the monastery, I would have ongoing access to Thomas Merton's guidance in his role as master of novices. For having experienced how transformative it had been to hear God speaking to me in Merton's writings, I could only imagine how wonderful it was going to be to receive spiritual guidance from Merton in ongoing face-to-face sessions of spiritual direction.

When I got to the monastery, I discovered that my hoped-for opportunity to receive personal guidance from Thomas Merton was not going to happen. The reason was that Thomas Merton was novice master of the choir novices who chanted the Psalms in Latin and who would go on to ordination in the priesthood. But because I was entering the monastery as a lay brother novice, I would be receiving spiritual guidance from the novice master of the lay brother novices.

This does not mean that I had no access to Thomas Merton. Each Sunday afternoon Thomas Merton gave a conference before Vespers to the choir and lay brother novices as well as to any professed members of the community who wanted to attend. It was very moving for me to be in the presence of Thomas Merton, whose writings had sustained me in the traumatizing events of my high school years. To experience directly for myself that he was real and that I was there with him listening to his voice left me feeling grateful and amazed. Merton said things in these talks that were sometimes funny, sometimes earthy, and always rich with experiential wisdom in the things of God.

In one of these conferences, he said something that deepened my sense of inner peace and resolve in my life as a lay brother novice. He spoke to us saying that we came to the monastery with high hopes for spiritual wisdom and fulfillment. And we are going around disgruntled in discovering once we got in here, that half of those living in here are crazy. We laughed because we knew he was referring to members of the community who were clearly not models of spiritual wisdom and mental health. The playwright Eugene O'Neill says somewhere that wherever human beings gather, there are layers upon layers of nonsense. Merton was, in effect, saying that in a cloistered monastery you will find layer upon layer of cloistered nonsense intermingled with a depth of wisdom and holiness beyond compare.

Merton went on to say that in the midst of our disgruntled ways we see an old lay brother coming toward us down the cloister like a transparent child, and we know he found what we came here hoping to find. Hearing Merton say this helped me to understand why I felt so at home in the simplicity of my life as a lay brother, which seemed by its very nature to render me childlike and transparent in the presence of God. At this stage of my life in the monastery I felt safe, grateful, and amazed in knowing in my heart that I was where God had so mysteriously led me and wanted me to be.

In one of Merton's Sunday afternoon talks he spoke to us of the mystery of creation revealed in the opening words of the Book of Genesis in which God's "let there be light" (Gen 1:1) speaks light into being, thus setting in motion God speaking all things into being.

Merton encouraged us to realize that God did not speak the world into existence and then go off to let the world get by as best it could on its own. For God's self-donating creative act is going on all the time. In each passing moment of our lives God is speaking us and all things into being.

Pondering the ongoing mystery of creation in this way led me to pray in a new way. I would sit in the silence of the vast interior of the monastic church, or I would walk out into the woods where I would sit at the base of a tree, asking God to help me to become so silent that I could hear God speaking me and all things into being. During the night I would lie on my straw mattress in the dark, asking God to help me to become so silent that I could hear God speaking me into being as I fell off to sleep.

This way of praying was greatly enhanced by the rule of silence in which we did not speak to one another. We used a simple monastic sign language to communicate necessary information. It is not that I did not speak at all. Each week I went to confession to one of the choir monks who was a priest from whom I could receive counsel in the sacrament of penance. Every other week I spoke with the novice master of lay brother novices in an ongoing process of discerning if the monastic life was my calling, my vocation from God. And I spoke once a month with the abbot in the ritual in which I entered his office, offered him a profound bow, and knelt on the floor at his desk to receive his guidance.

What contributed to the pervasive quality of the silence was that there were no recreation periods in which we could talk and get to know one another. Nor were we allowed to write notes to one another. The monastic lore at the time was that a novice asked the abbot if we could have recreation periods so that we could talk to one another to better understand one another. The abbot responded, saying there would be no recreation periods, telling the novice that we did not come to the monastery to understand one another, but rather to believe in one another.

During the nearly six years I lived in the monastery, I did not speak in any kind of casual conversational way with the men I was living with day by day. Nor did any of them speak to me. I was a silent God-seeking young man in a community of silent God-seeking men. Living in this perpetual silence had a profound and lasting effect on me, for which I am immensely grateful.

Chanting the Psalms throughout the day helped me to realize that there are words that disturb the God-laden silence and there are words that resonate and embody what is hidden and given in silence. For when we stood together chanting the Psalms, we were chanting God's words revealed to us in scripture that God is one with us as we really are with all our anger, our fears, our confusion, our hopes and longings that stir within us in the presence of God sustaining us and guiding us to God just as we are.

The pervasive silence was especially evident on Sundays. The schedule on Sundays was the same as every day of the week. We still got up at 2:30 in the morning, and we chanted the Psalms for seven canonical hours throughout the day. The difference was that there was no manual labor. So we had all day to live in silence with nothing to do but pray, to visit the cemetery with its row upon row of crosses marking the graves of the monks who had gone on before us into God, to take long walks in the woods that surrounded the monastery, to become absorbed in the reading of scripture and other spiritual reading, or simply to sit in silence surrendered over the eternal silence of God.

In one of his journal entries Merton describes Sunday afternoons in the monastery, writing: "The young monks lean sadly against walls, asking questions that have no answers. The old monks are silent because they have given up interest in speech." To lean sadly up against walls asking questions that have no answer is its own, more interior kind of silence, in which any answer to whatever question you might ask will, in being finite, not be what you are looking for.

An amazing effect of being immersed in this endless silence is that the least little thing can suddenly lay bare the God-given Godly nature of whatever we might be aware of. Merton writes of one such moment that was granted to him as he was sitting alone in silence when "suddenly the silence was broken by the song of a bird announcing the difference between heaven and hell." Being interiorly quickened and accessed by God in this way is a taste of heaven. And compared to that celestial state of interior clarity, our estrangement from

God's all-encompassing presence has about it the feeling of being lost in the outer fringes of hell, in which we go about searching this way and that for the Beloved without whom we know our lives will be forever incomplete. And it is in surrendering ourselves over to these ever so subtle longings that the Beloved heals us of all that hinders us from realizing that the Beloved is always there and ever shall be there, as the very reality of our longings and of each passing moment of our lives, come what may.

Later on, as I continued in my spiritual practices after I left the monastery, I came to realize that, yes, it is true that out here in the midst of the world we are surrounded by all sorts of noise and superficial chatter that can intrude upon our sense of inner peace and God's presence in our lives. But it is also true that we can learn to listen to the sound of the wind and the song of birds and the laughter of children and many other sounds as well that renew our spirits and restore us to a more grounded sense of ourselves in God's presence. And, then too, there are the words of lovers and poets and the words of those who cry out in their suffering, asking for help, and the words of those who seek to offer help as best they can, all bearing witness to and embodying God's oneness with us in life itself. I hope that you are sensing in these reflections some words that echo with the ways you are being led so unexplainably along your own experience of the healing path we are exploring together in these reflections.

My daily life of silence and prayer in the monastery left me feeling amazed and grateful to have been led by God into such simplicity and blessedness. That is why I was so blindsided and upset by a seemingly simple event that reawakened the traumatized self that I thought I had left behind when I entered the monastery.

The seemingly simple incident that brought this about occurred when I saw a notice thumbtacked to the bulletin board in the lay brothers' novitiate. The typed notice, which I can still see in my mind's eye, said: *Professor Danial Walsh is beginning first year philosophy classes for the choir novices beginning their studies for the priesthood. Any lay brother novice who wants to sit in on the class for personal enrichment can do so by signing up below.*

Without even knowing what philosophy was, I signed up to sit in on the class because I knew, from having read Merton's autobiography, *The Seven Storey Mountain*, that Dan Walsh had taught medieval philosophy at Columbia University when the young Thomas Merton was a student there and going through the graced tumult of religious conversion that led him into the Catholic Church. I knew that it was Dan Walsh who encouraged the young Thomas Merton to make his fateful visit to Gethsemani, which led him to enter the monastery.

It was in this spirit that I signed up to sit in on the class, free of any concerns that I might not be smart enough to understand philosophy. I simply wanted to be in the presence of Dan Walsh, whose fidelity to his own calling as a professor of philosophy led him to play a providential role in helping Merton to be faithful to his calling to be a monk and to write the books that inspired me to be faithful to my calling to enter the monastery.

Almost immediately after signing up for the class, I began to feel upset, as it suddenly occurred to me that Dan Walsh might call on me in class. It was only in some obscure way that I realized being asked to speak in the presence of the choir novices beginning their studies for the priesthood would be disturbingly similar to what it felt like when I was in ninth grade, feeling painfully exposed as too dumb to pass Latin and algebra and other college preparatory courses in the midst of students who were passing these courses with apparent ease.

By the time I went to sleep that night, my sense of inner peace in the presence of God was nowhere to be found, so overtaken was I with anxiety. I took myself to task in wondering how I could have been so stupid as to get myself into this disturbing situation in which the choir novices would see how stupid I was if Dan Walsh called on me in class to speak.

That night I had a nightmare in which I dreamed I was sitting in a circle with the choir novices with whom I would be sitting in Dan Walsh's philosophy class. I had a large tablet on my lap on which Dan Walsh had asked me to write the word *the* with a large black marker. Not knowing how to spell the word *the,* I wrote *tha.* At which point the choir novices started laughing at me. Feeling suddenly exposed and ashamed, I scratched out what I had written and, in an attempt to salvage the situation, wrote *thi,* causing them to laugh harder. In an increasingly more frantic state, I scratched out *thi* and wrote *tho,* causing them to laugh harder, triggering such intense feelings of annihilating shame that I screamed in my sleep, waking myself up.

The instant that I awoke and realized where I was and what had just happened, I felt embarrassed in knowing that my scream had probably awakened those sleeping around me in their partitioned-off cubicles in the common dormitory. At a deeper level, as I lay there on my straw mattress with my heart pounding from the self-annihilating feelings of the nightmare, I knew within myself that the terror the nightmare had triggered in me was the very same terror I felt when I was a preschooler, lying in my bed in the dark, listening to my father beat my mother just outside my bedroom.

Only now my situation was much worse than when I was a preschooler. For then, lying there in the dark,

God's presence mysteriously emerged out of my fear and sadness, letting me know that God was present, sustaining me in the midst of my difficulties. But now that I had entered the monastery the situation was reversed. For now, instead of the light of God emerging out of the darkness, the darkness of traumatizing terror and sadness was emerging out of the atmospheric light and safety of my God-filled life in the monastery. It let me know, in some primitive, body-grounded way that I was still a traumatized child wearing monks' robes.

The bell rang at 2:30 the next morning, letting me know it was time to chant the Psalms for Vigils in English in lay brother novice chapel. I stood there chanting the words of the Psalms, but I could not pray because I was so overwhelmed by feelings of traumatizing anxiety. Searching within myself for some way out of my dilemma, it occurred to me that one option was simply not to go to the class. But because everything had to be done under obedience, I would have to go to my novice master for permission to not attend the class. And this I knew I could not do because he might ask me to tell him why I had changed my mind.

For you see, through my four years of high school in which I was writing regularly to the vocation director, Father John of the Cross, of my desire to enter the monastery, I never mentioned the ongoing traumatizing violence I was living in day by day. The same was true after I arrived at the monastery when I was interviewed by Father John Eudes. Seeing that I had just turned eighteen years old and just a week earlier had graduated from high school, he wanted to know what my parents thought of my desire to enter the monastery. I lied in indicating that they were fine with it. I did not tell him about my father's violence. Nor did I mention that because my mother's Catholicism was one of the themes that triggered my father's rage, I had not told him about my desire to enter the monastery until just a few days after graduating from high school. And I was especially careful not tell Father John Eudes that when I told my father that I wanted to enter the monastery, he told me that if I went to the monastery, he would murder my mother to punish me. In the previous chapter I have explained my reasons, especially the fact that I had so thoroughly dissociated my ongoing internalized trauma out of my conscious awareness that I did not know I was traumatized.

It is as if you were born with red lenses in your eyes, so that everything you saw would be red. This, in turn, without you realizing it, would distort every color that you saw. Ever since I was a small child I saw myself and everyone around me through traumatized eyes. And so I was not able consciously to know that I was traumatized. All this was why I intuited in some obscure way that I could not ask my novice master's permission not to attend the philosophy class, for that would require telling him the shame-based secret of the trauma that I was still keeping from myself.

Please notice how I have been sharing my fears of being called on in the philosophy class and the nightmare my fears evoked in a slow motion, detailed kind of way that corresponds to the interior sense of slow-motion time in which my reawakened feelings of trauma lived on within me and were now invading the holy silence that I had only just begun to savor.

When the day for the first lecture in the philosophy class arrived, I joined the ten or so choir novices and the one other lay brother novice who had signed up to sit in on the class. As we sat there in silence waiting for Dan Walsh to arrive, my calm exterior masked the anticipatory anxiety in which I was hoping and praying that Dan Walsh would not call on me.

Dan Walsh began with introductory comments that I but scarcely remember and only vaguely understood as having to do with the fact that we were going to begin with the field of cosmology by focusing on the teachings of Saint Thomas Aquinas on the ontological, spiritual dimensions of the material world.

What I keenly remember is the moment Dan Walsh began to get into the substance of his lecture by holding up his pen and saying, "This pen is like every pen in this room in that it is a pen." I remember, as I wrote that down, thinking to myself, "That's true." Still holding up his pen, he said, "This pen is like every pen in the world in that it is a pen." Surprised by the sudden expansion of the truth of what he was saying, extending out into the whole world, I wrote that down, sensing within myself an unexpected joy and relief that I was able to understand what he was saying in some self-evident kind of way. He then said, "This pen is like everything in this room in that it is a thing, and this pen is like everything in the world in that it a thing." As he spoke, his words continued to evoke my silent, interior Yes, yes, how true, how true.

Then holding up his pen a little higher and with more emphasis in his voice, he said, "And yet, out of all the pens in this room, all the pens in the world, out of all the things in this room, all the things in world, only this pen is *this* pen. Therefore, there must be in this pen a principle of likeness and a principle of difference."

And I fell off my chair. Not literally, of course, but interiorly, for in that moment I discovered for the first time in my life that I had a mind. And at a more expansive scale, I was amazed to discover that the philosophical theology of the Middle Ages provides a way of speaking of the ultimate, divine dimensions of the mystery of what it means to be.

With guidance from Dan Walsh's lectures I began the challenging and rewarding process of reading the writings of Saint Augustine and Saint Thomas Aquinas, aided by commentaries by the contemporary Thomistic philosophers Etienne Gilson, Jacques Maritain, Josef Pieper, and others. I was also introduced to and deeply affected by the writings of the contemporary philosopher Gabriel Marcel and the poetic elegance of Max Picard's *World of Silence*.

I then decided that I wanted to learn Latin so that I could read Thomas Aquinas's *Summa Theologica* in Latin. Much to my surprise I became bold enough to raise my hand in class and ask Dan Walsh questions. Once I asked, "Could we say that after the geographical Tokyo no longer exists there will there still be Tokyo?" He said, "Yes. Because Tokyo is in God's mind and God never forgets, which is why in the ultimate spiritual order of things everything real is forever." To appreciate the practical relevance of such an understanding to us here, we can ponder what it means to say that when you and I die and cross over into God, we will cross over into the eternality of this moment in which you and I are reading and writing these words in God in whom all that is passing away eternally subsists.

A few days after taking my first essay exam in Dan Walsh's class, the novice master of the lay brother novices called me into his office. He told me that the abbot, in having read my exam, wanted me to change from the brothers' novitiate into the choir novitiate.

My novice master asked, "Are you willing to do that?" As stunned as I was in hearing this, I had no trouble in immediately saying yes, I was willing to do that. "Good," he said, "get your things and take them over to the choir novitiate. They are expecting you." And so I gathered up my things, which really amounted to my Bible, a ballpoint pen, and my personal notes. I left the lay brothers' novitiate building and walked the short distance across the monastic enclosure to the main monastic building. I walked down what they called the little cloister and into the choir novitiate, with its own chapel, scriptorium, small library, and conference room.

The next morning, when I awoke at 2:30, instead of going upstairs to the small chapel of the lay brothers' novitiate to chant the Psalms for Vigils in English, I went to the monastic church to join the choir monks in chanting the Psalms for Vigils in Latin. The essentials of my daily life were the same. I was still following what I believed to be my vocation of seeking God in silence and prayer, but now my monastic vocation would include the prayerful study of scripture, philosophy, and the writings of the monastic fathers, which would eventually lead to taking solemn vows and being ordained to the priesthood.

Best of all, I knew that what I dreamed of in high school was going to come true. I was going to be with Thomas Merton as my novice master in ongoing sessions of one-on-one spiritual direction in which he was going to help me find my way into the secret of God's face. Little did I know that as I learned to gaze into the secret of God's face, I would discover it to be a mirror, reflecting back to me who God eternally knows and calls me to be in the midst of all that remained unresolved in my mind and heart.

May each of us learn to be healed from all that hinders us from realizing, as we gaze into the secret of God's face, that we are gazing into a mirror reflecting back to us who God eternally knows and calls us to be in the midst of all that remains unresolved in our minds and hearts.

Amen. So be it.

6

From the Pig Barn to the Sheep Barn and Beyond

In the choir novitiate they posted the name of the novice who was scheduled the following day for his one-on-one session of spiritual direction with Thomas Merton. The first time I saw my name posted, I was happy in knowing that my dream of having Thomas Merton guide me into the secret of God's face was about to come true.

I do not remember how my first session with Thomas Merton began. I know we would have followed the ritual in which I said "Benedicite," with its intended Latin equivalent for saying, "Give me a blessing to speak." Merton would then have said "Dominus," which is Latin for "Lord," with its implied meaning, "May the Lord bless our conversation." I am assuming that I began by telling him that I worked in the farrowing barn, where the sows had their litters. And he, no doubt, wanted to know about how I felt in moving over from the brothers into the choir novitiate. What I keenly remember is how small and insignificant I felt compared to how holy and famous Merton was to me and to many others all over the world who, like me, had been inspired in reading his books on the spiritual life. I felt like I was in the presence of some towering figure, like Moses, coming down from the mountain, with his face shining bright with the glory of God. I was so overcome by feelings of inadequacy that I began to hyperventilate, as I became too nervous to speak in a clear and coherent way.

Seeing how anxious I was, he asked, "What's going on?" With my voice shaking I said, "I am afraid because you are Thomas Merton." This wasn't at all the way I had hoped and imagined this long-anticipated moment was going to be. I so wanted Thomas Merton to think well of me. And now, much to my dismay, the opposite was happening, for now he could see the terrified me I so wanted not to be.

Then something amazing happened. Instead of commenting on my anxiety, he said, in a calm and reassuring voice, "Under obedience I want you, each day, to end afternoon work a bit early so that you can come here to my office before Vespers to tell me one thing that happened that day at the pig barn." As soon as he said that, I could feel my anxiety drain out of my body as I could hear the voice inside of me silently say, "We can do that!"

And so each day I would end work a bit early, change from my work clothes into my monastic habit and go to his office. We would say our "Benedicite" and "Dominus." Then I would tell him something that happened that day at the pig barn. He remembered the things I had shared. He would ask, "How's that sow with the injured foot doing? Is she getting better?" And he would make me laugh, with jokes and observations about pigs and about some of the members of the community and about life in general. It was in these encounters that Merton, without saying so directly, was mentoring me in discovering for myself that it is in humility and mercy that we begin to find our way into the secret of God's face.

I must say that out of everything I have learned from prayerfully exploring Thomas Merton's teachings over the years, nothing has affected me more deeply than the wisdom and compassion in which he, in hearing me say, "I am afraid because your are Thomas Merton," responded in such a simple and compassionate way and allowed me to feel relaxed and comfortable in his presence. In this way he freed me up to share with him the sincere longing for God that drew me to the monastery.

It was not long after I had changed over into the choir novitiate that I noticed an abandoned sheep barn that I could see from the window in the choir novitiate scriptorium. One day while out walking, I inspected the abandoned sheep barn. Entering through the open door on the ground floor, I climbed the ladder that went up into the loft. One wall of the loft was stacked high with bales of straw that I assumed were used by the lay brothers who managed the dairy herd. Along another wall was a large open door that opened out upon the woods leading up a hill to the hermitage, where Merton had just been given permission to spend some time each day. And at a slight angle to those trees was a clear view of a meadow and in the distance the wooded hills and bottom lands of the monastery's vast expanse of land. As I sat on a bail of straw near the open loft door, praying and gazing at the meadow, I immediately sensed that this would be a wonderful place where I could come each day to pray.

The next time I went to see Thomas Merton for spiritual direction, I asked his permission to spend some time each day alone in the loft of the sheep barn. With Merton's permission, I began my daily ritual of going to the loft of the sheep barn to pray and be alone with God.

One day as I walked back and forth in the loft of the barn reading the Psalms, I began to realize that what we tend to think of as the air is actually God. In a subtle, interior way I sensed that I was walking back and forth in the atmospheric, all-encompassing presence of God, who was sustaining me breath by breath. I can recall realizing that if I were to try to flee from the atmospheric, all-encompassing presence of God that, no matter where I would flee to, God would be sustaining me in my flight from God, and that wherever my arrival point might be, God would be waiting for me when I got there.

The peace that came over me in this divinized state flowed from a deep realization that there was no need to flee from God's all-encompassing presence. For the most intimate depth of this awakening moment was a simple awareness that God, who was sustaining my life breath by breath, knew me through and through as mercy within mercy within mercy. I was so overtaken by the intimate depths of my very presence being accessed by the presence of God in this way that I stopped reading the Psalms and simply sat on a bail of straw breathing God as I looked out over the meadow.

As I sat there, a pair of barn swallows that had built their nest in the barn were swooping this way and that over the meadow. From time to time one of the red wasps that were part of the landscape in the hot summers of Kentucky would come flying into the loft, pause in midair for just a moment to get its bearings, and then ascend, like a helicopter, up into the rafters of the barn, where the wasps were building the mud nests in which they laid their eggs.

What was even more amazing is that this graced awareness of God and I inhaling and exhaling ourselves into each other continued for the next three days. It's not that I walked around in some kind of trance. Quite the opposite, actually, in that I felt very present to each thing that I did throughout the day, but present in a pervasive underlying awareness of being in the presence of God, sustaining me breath by breath, knowing me through and through with an infused sense of mercy without end.

The third day of my God-breathing way of life fell on a Sunday, which was the one day of the week we were allowed to walk in the woods on the other side of the small, winding country road that cut through the monastery property. I crossed the road and walked along the narrow dirt path as it turned to the right, and then to the left, and began its gentle ascent up through woods to Dom Frederick's Lake, where I would go on Sundays to sit and pray.

As I walked along that narrow dirt path with its overarching canopy of trees, I paused and touched a leaf hanging from a low-lying branch. As I touched the leaf, I looked up and saw a single cloud hanging in the clear blue sky and whispered, "It's one!" The infinite presence of God I was breathing, the cloud in the sky, the leaf I was touching, the earth on which I was standing, and the immediacy of feeling myself blessed and awakened to this all-encompassing presence were, in that instant, realized to be inexplicably and all-pervasively one. Please know that the words I am using in attempting to describe this intimately realized oneness are impoverished in a superficial, wordy kind of way compared to the transcendent oneness beyond words that I was so graced and privileged to experience.

Moved by the all-encompassing presence in which I was immersed, I walked off the path onto a field, where I sat in the tall grass moved by a strong wind with the blue sky overhead, all of which were experienced as bodying forth the endless diversity of the oneness of presence that alone is ultimately real.

As I share this memory with you now, more than fifty years later, I can honestly say that my life since that moment has never been quite the same. For even though I have drifted many times from my direct awareness of this all-encompassing oneness, the all-encompassing presence of God has never drifted away from me. It is so strange how grace can flow so quietly in the secret recesses of those, such as myself, who are so limited in so many ways.

In my next session of spiritual direction I asked Thomas Merton to help me to understand and to be faithful to these transformative experiences that were so new to me. I do not remember how he responded to all that I was sharing. But what I clearly remember and took to heart was the quiet assurance with which he said: "Once in a while you will find someone with whom you can talk about such things. But they are hard to find. And when you are fortunate enough to find such a person it will be a temporary arrangement. For you will spend most of your life without such a person, which will be your solitude in which you will learn from God how to depend on God to guide you into ever deeper communion with God."

In saying this to me, he must have known that I saw him as the person with whom I was in that very moment speaking of such things. He must have known that I believed with all my heart that I had been providentially led by God to this very moment in which my longstanding dream of having him guide me into the secret of God's face was coming true. In his role as my novice master, Merton accepted me into his graces and began to guide me in the art of learning to be supple and responsive to the mysterious process in which God and I kept yielding ourselves over into each other. I think it was in moments such as these that Merton tried to help me appreciate that the monastic life that we were both living had been carefully crafted by Saint Benedict as a way to follow Christ in prayerful silence

and poverty of spirit that invites this mystical communion with God that foreshadows our eternal destiny in
paradise.

One Sunday winter afternoon in which snow had
been falling throughout the day I walked in the woods
to Dom Frederick's Lake where I would go to sit and
pray. I sat in the snow at the base of a tree. I put my
head back against the tree and gazed up through the
bare branches as the snow kept falling from unseen
places in a slate gray sky. It was so silent that I could
hear the subtle *sssssst* sound of the snow falling on the
crust of snow that covered the ground.

As I sat there, still as stone, a full-grown deer came
walking past me, not more than twenty feet from where
I sat! Pausing for just a moment, the deer turned and
looked at me, head full of antlers, eyes full of God. But
so still was I that he looked right at me but did not
see me. Then the majestic buck continued on its way,
disappearing into the woods.

As I continued sitting there, looking upward, I
prayed, without words, asking from within myself,
"Lord, is this the way it is with us? In looking up
through these bare branches, seeing the snow falling
from the lead gray sky, am I looking right at you, but
I don't see you?"

And yet in the depths of my heart I see you seeing
me, giving yourself to me so unexplainably in and as

these bare branches and in the snow falling, falling, falling, with its secret whisper of your presence. Sitting there in the snow I could hear in the distance the monastery bell letting me know that I had to return to chant Vespers. There were many moments like this for me that flowed out, now here, now there, in the pervasive silence and simplicity of my life in the monastery.

As a way to end this chapter I share with you a poetic meditation by inviting you to imagine that a magician is fanning out a deck of cards face down on a table and says, "Go ahead, pick a card, any card, and then bury it facedown back in the deck." It does not matter which card you choose. The magician will bring it forth from your shirt pocket or, perhaps, from behind your ear.

Now imagine you are out walking on the beach and God says, "Go ahead, pick a grain of sand, any grain." Because God is not subject to division or diminishment of any kind, no matter which grain of sand you choose, God will be completely present—in that one little grain of sand. Furthermore, since the whole universe flows from God, is sustained by God, and subsists in God, you are holding in your hand a grain of sand in which you, along with the whole universe and everyone and everything in it, is unexplainably present in that one little grain of sand.

Surprised by such an all-encompassing oneness, you begin to get a little weak in the knees. Then God moves in to finish you off by suddenly expanding this awareness of realized oneness in all directions. "Go ahead," God says, "pick a place, a situation, a circumstance in which you might find yourself." If you choose a wooded area, you see yourself in your mind's eye surrounded by trees. God is there, inviting you to reach out and touch a leaf on a low-lying branch. As you do so, you realize you are touching a leaf in which the totality of God is wholly present. If you choose your own home, God is there, inviting you to choose something, anything at all: the tea kettle on the stove, or perhaps a chair in a corner of the living room. No matter what you might choose, you realize you are choosing something in which God is wholly present, loving you, and all people, and all things, into being.

Then God invites you to reflect on any aspect of yourself. No matter what aspect of yourself you focus on, God is there, wholly present in each breath, each thought, each feeling, each turn of your head. You realize that as you sit, God is present as the ungraspable immediacy of your sitting. As you stand, God is present in the ungraspable immediacy of your standing. As you laugh, God is there as your laughter. As you cry, God is wholly present in each tear falling from your eyes.

It does not matter what little thing you might choose, within or around you. It might just be the thing that awakens you from your fitful dream of being separate from God, who is the reality of yourself and all that is real.

May we be so blessed as to be finished off by God, swooping down from above, welling up from beneath, to extinguish the illusion of separateness that perpetuates our fears. May we, in having our illusory, separate self slain by God, be born into a new and true awareness of who we really are, one with God forever. May we continue on in this true awareness, seeing in each and every little thing we see, the fullness of God's presence in our lives. May we learn to be someone in whose presence others are better able to recognize God's presence in their lives, so that they, too, might know the freedom of the children of God.

Amen. So be it.

7

Refuge

During my novitiate the prayerful silence of the monastic life, the chanting of the Psalms, and my one-on-one sessions with Thomas Merton continued to be my primary sources of spiritual guidance and support. In accordance with the customs of the monastery, I also had access to spiritual guidance from a priest in the community that I chose to go to each week to hear my confession.

I liked the confessor I was going to each week, but then a choir monk who had been away in his studies in Rome returned to the monastery. When he spoke to the community I was impressed by his sense of spiritual presence and his quality of mind. And so I asked Thomas Merton for permission to change from my present confessor to this other priest. Thomas Merton gladly agreed and told me how impressed he was with this priest and pleased that I would be receiving guidance from him as my confessor.

The ritual for weekly confession was simple enough. Once a week after chanting Vespers and having a simple supper eaten in silence with the community, I would go to the church and kneel off to the side waiting for the priest to arrive who was to hear my confession. I would follow him along the row of small alcoves behind the high altar of the monastic church. In each alcove there was a small kneeler, above which was a wooden grill in the wall. The priest would sit on one side, with his ear toward the grill. I would kneel on the other side of the wooden grill, through which I would sincerely confess such things as daydreaming and not really praying when chanting Psalms in the monastic choir, having uncharitable thoughts about someone in the community, or not being responsible for my daily duties working at the pig barn. Before receiving absolution for these spiritual imperfections, I was free to ask whatever questions and concerns were weighing on me at the time. It was in these talks that I noticed that, while Merton's insights were always clear and sincere, my new confessor's responses seemed more emotionally sincere, conveying to me that he cared about me at the feeling level.

It was in the alliance formed in my weekly interactions with my confessor that I felt safe enough to tell him about my father's traumatizing violence toward my mother, my younger siblings, and myself, and how disturbing and confusing these experiences were to me. The priest responded to these self-disclosures in a very understanding and supportive way by saying how terrible it must have been for me to go through those experiences and how mysterious it was that God had led me out of that violence and into the peace and safety of the monastery.

As time went by, my weekly time with the priest became the emotional center for my week. Looking back at this now, I realize that his support and understanding meant so much to me because I experienced him as being the loving and understanding father I never had growing up at home. He was tall and thin like my father, but unlike my father, the priest was gentle and kind. I trusted him and sensed that he sincerely cared about me. And so the emotional support and spiritual guidance I was receiving from the priest each week in confession was for me another grace that was woven into the fabric of blessings that made up my daily life in the monastery.

It went on this way for more than a year. Then, during one of my weekly sessions of receiving spiritual guidance and support from the priest in confession, he told me that he believed that Our Lord had providentially graced us with our very special relationship.

He told me there was a room where we could have the privacy we needed to explore our relationship further. He said that night, when the community ended the day by chanting the Psalms of Compline and would be going in silence to their cells in the dormitory, I should instead go to a room where he had arranged for us to meet. He asked if I was willing to do that. Confused and surprised by what he was asking me to do, I whispered, "Yes." He said, "Good." As I stood up to leave, I remember him saying, "Be discreet," by which I understood him to mean I should be careful that no one saw me enter the room where he would be waiting for me. As I knelt in the church to say the prayers he had given me for my penance, my head was spinning in not being able to take in what had just happened, or what was going to happen when I went to the room where he told me he would be waiting for me.

When I entered the room where the priest was waiting, he was very happy to see me. Then something terrible happened. He told me that we should begin by taking off our clothes. As we each took off our monastic habit, I was shaking because I was so nervous and confused about what was happening. He wanted me to have sex with him. But I am not gay. I did not want to hurt his feelings or even worse make him mad at me, but it just wasn't in me to kiss him or do the sexual things he wanted me to do to him. And so I let him have sex with me.

When it was over, I fell into the numb place that was strangely similar to the numb place I would go into at home when I knew my father might hit me at any moment and there was nothing I could do to stop it. When the priest saw I had become so strangely quiet and still, he kept asking if I was ok. I kept nodding my head, indicating I was ok. As I stood up and put on my monastic habit, the only thing I could say over and over was, "I need to go. I need to go."

I can remember walking alone down the long corridor that led from that room to my cell in the dormitory. I closed the curtain on my cell and lay down on the straw mattress. It was the loneliest and most confusing night of my whole life.

The next morning when the bell rang at 2:30 for me to wake up to chant the Psalms for Vigils I could tell that I felt fine in the disturbingly familiar way that I felt fine at home, where I had learned to walk about as the ghost that other people could see as a way of hiding the terrified me that nobody could see. What felt so strange and disturbing was to find myself walking about in the prayerful silence of the monastery in the same dissociative survival mode I had lived in as a child.

The rule of communal silence provided a safety net that protected me from having to engage with the priest until the following week when the time came for him to hear my confession. He told me that he had been concerned about me all week because of how upset I was that last time we were together. I told him that I was fine. He told me that for him our private time together confirmed how special and graced our relationship with each other really was and that he realized how important it was for us to continue exploring our very special friendship in that way. Not knowing that I was allowed to or even capable of disagreeing with him, I told him that I felt the same way. From that moment on the external pattern and rhythm of my daily life in the monastery was interspersed with the priest letting me know in confession that the time had come for us to meet in the secret place to continue exploring the very special relationship that Our Lord had given us.

Once again I found myself in the inner world of my childhood, where I knew firsthand that there is no place so safe as being a child in one's own home, or, as was now the case, no place so pure and innocent as a cloistered monastery, that traumatizing forces could not find me and bring me down. This was especially devastating for me in realizing that I was passively going along with the destructive forces that were bringing me down.

These realizations would have left me in despair were it not for my heart knowledge, born of faith, that the darkness of this world has no refuge from the presence of God, which protects us from nothing, even as it inexplicably sustains us amid the trials and tribulations of this world.

The challenge lies in the extent to which the intensity of traumatizing events can close off our experiential access to God's sustaining presence. The grace lies in the ways in which the light of God's presence begins to shine ever so meekly in the darkness in which we have lost our way. The grace deepens as we learn to follow the light out of the darkness, leading us on and on, as we fall back again and again into the darkness, only to rise up again and again to follow the light into the light. The grace deepens still more as we learn to bring with us out into the light the lessons we learned in the darkness about the graced and mysterious wholeness that permeates our fragility when it is deeply accepted.

The grace deepens still more as we learn to discern and obey the promptings of our awakened heart to pass on to others the lessons we learned in the darkness. That, by the way, is what I am attempting to pass on to you in writing these reflections, hoping you might find here words of guidance and encouragement in your own healing journey, whatever the conditions and circumstances of your own healing journey might be.

I am now going to share with you how the deepening layers of my passivity and secrecy in my relationship
with the priest reawakened and mirrored the traumatizing effects of passivity and secrecy in my relationship
with my father. Then I will share how I discovered in
the land of the lost that God has secrets of God's own
that quietly illumined and sustained me, even as I continued to unravel and fall apart.

As I reflect back to the patterns of passivity in my
relationship with my father that most directly mirrors
my passivity with the priest, what first comes to mind
is a particularly painful moment that occurred when I
was a senior in high school, just a few months before I
left home to come to the monastery.

I came home late one night after being out with my
friends. My mother and my younger siblings had all gone
to bed. My father was alone in the kitchen, obviously
very drunk. I had learned to avoid being alone with him
when he had been drinking, but now, all of a sudden,
there we were together in the kitchen. In the rambling,
slurred way he would talk when he was drunk, he told
me to sit down, and he began to tell me in a very angry
way how ashamed he was that I was his son.

Becoming increasingly angry, he stood up and yelled
at me to stand up. When I stood up, he pushed me very
hard on my chest, knocking me backward onto the
floor. He stood over me with his fists clenched, yelling

at me to stand up. When I stood up, he again knocked me to the floor. This continued on, beginning in the kitchen, and on through the dining room, and into the living room, where I ended up on the floor with him standing over me, yelling at me to stand up, while I just lay there until eventually he walked away. When he had gone back into the kitchen, I got up off the floor and walked upstairs to my bedroom, feeling utterly ashamed that my father was so ashamed of me.

Looking back at this moment I think that if instead of passively letting my father repeatedly knock me to the floor I had screamed at him to stop, or hit him, or tried to knock him to the floor, he would have burst out laughing and would have given me a hug, proudly satisfied that he had not failed to make a man of me, just as his own father had made a man out of him. But in my traumatized self I dared not risk even thinking that I was capable of stepping forward on my own behalf, for to do so meant taking the risk that he might, in his drunken rage, murder me.

What was so deeply regrettable about the priest sexualizing the trust I placed in his loving concern for me was that he was the first person who loved me and cared about me and saw me, not just in the sunlit realms of my soul open to God, but as the immature and traumatized young adult that I had shared so openly with him as my confessor. And so I could not bear to let myself think for a moment that he was doing anything that was not in his priestly wisdom what he knew and believed to be what I needed in my ongoing search for God.

Every little boy needs a daddy and if, as a small child and on through my adolescence, the only daddy I had was the daddy who was beating me, I accepted that as the painful option that was not as terrifying as having no daddy at all. This is the dilemma of traumatized children, knowing they cannot survive without the parent who is destroying them. In having carried this traumatized inner child with me into the monastery, I viscerally believed within myself that if the only spiritual father who saw me and cared about me at the feeling level was the priest who was having sex with me, then, as disorienting as that was, it was not as terrifying as losing the wise guidance of the learned priest and man of prayer who saw me and cared about me at the feeling level.

A troubling grace stirred within me as I came to realize that I was no longer the traumatized little boy who still lived within me. For I was now a young man living at the edge of a precipice of knowing that if God loved me and cherished me as real and lovable in his eyes, I could not pretend that I was not the real person God loved and called me to be. I could not be true to God and at the same time give in to fears that prevented me from setting boundaries with anyone, whether my father or the priest or anyone else for that matter who was treating me in ways that were unworthy of how I deep down knew I deserved to be treated.

It was in this humbling realization that I lacked the strength to do what I knew I had to do in confronting the priest's inappropriate and destructive behavior that I began to worry that I was an imposter pretending that I was following the spiritual path when interiorly I had perhaps already strayed so far off the path that I did not know if I could find my way back again.

In some strange way I could not understand, it seemed that just as my passivity traumatically bonded me to my father, so, too, my passivity traumatically bonded me to the priest.

It was in the midst of this road to nowhere that I began to sense that God was inviting me to give up trying to overcome my fear and to instead bring my feelings of fear and shame to Jesus. I was already committed in my heart to follow the directive of Saint Benedict in his Rule that the monk should "prefer nothing to Christ." But at this point I needed to go beyond a theological understanding of the universality of Christ by praying my way into the deathless presence of Jesus.

The felt need to pray in this way led me to imagine, as in a kind of waking dream, that I was alone on a moonlit night in the garden where the Gospels tell us Jesus would go to spend whole nights alone in prayer. In my mind's eye I could see and feel myself searching here and there, looking for Jesus so that I might share with him how powerless I was to be true to who I sensed he was calling me to be. I sensed, too, that Jesus knew I was there and that the rendezvous between us that was about to occur had been providentially prearranged.

Then suddenly, looking this way and that, I saw Jesus sitting alone in the moonlight at the edge of a clearing. I walked across the clearing and knelt at his feet. I could feel his hand on my shoulder as I leaned in close to whisper in his ear, revealing the burdens of my shame-based weakness and fear.

Having poured out all that my wounded and hurting heart was moved and able to say, Jesus drew me in close and whispered in my ear three words that set me free, words that still echo inside me to this day. I heard him whisper: "I love you!"

Dazed and amazed in being so unexplainably loved, the spirit within me let me know what both Jesus and I were waiting to hear me say. So I leaned in close and whispered my secret "I love you" to Jesus. And there in that instant there was the realization between us that the matter was settled once and for all. The matter being that the good news of God's love for us is never measured by our ability to be true to who we know in our heart God is calling us to be. For the sole measure of God's love for us is the measureless expanse of God's

merciful love, permeating us and taking us to itself in
the midst of our faltering and wayward ways.

As I began to take in the grace of this taste of experiential salvation, I realized that I had made three
mistakes. The first was that I had placed my faith in the
priest instead of in God. Second, I had placed my faith
in myself instead of in God. And third, I had failed to
realize that as lost as I had become, God had in no way
whatsoever lost sight of me. For God's merciful love
for me, for the priest, for my traumatizing father, and
for all of us is infinitely greater than our finite abilities and inabilities to be true to that love that alone is
ultimately real.

This liberating awakening did not bring with it the
courage to tell the priest what I needed to say, but my
healing encounter with Jesus allowed me to realize that
I was empowered to actively wait for God to achieve
in me what I, by my own finite and wounded abilities,
was powerless to achieve. The art of active waiting as
a spiritual practice consists of a willingness to do what
one needs to do when the grace to do it is given.

And so, I simply had to accept that I did not know
just how my breaking away from the priest as my confessor would occur. Perhaps I would suddenly blurt out
pent-up truths that I could not and would not want
to take back. Or perhaps the liberation would occur in

some unexpected event that would provide a break in the prison wall, allowing me to find my way to freedom.

The decisive moment of my deliverance occurred quite unexpectedly in a conversation the priest and I were having when he was hearing my confession. We were talking about my future and how, most likely, what was going to happen was that I would make solemn vows and get ordained to the priesthood. Most likely I would be sent to Rome for further studies and hopefully have the opportunity to study philosophy under the guidance of Father Bernard Lonergan, just as I currently studied under the guidance of Professor Daniel Walsh. And then the priest said quite casually that when I returned from Rome, he and I could pick up where we had left off in exploring the very special relationship God had given us.

Externally I agreed with his scenario of my future, but within myself I suddenly became extremely upset. The inner voice that speaks to me at such times, said, "He is not going to let us go." For up to that moment, I had been secretly hoping that he was going to move on and leave me alone. But now I knew that he had no intention of ever letting go of his claim on me in what he called our very special relationship.

Within hours of that conversation, I fell into a deep depression. I shifted interiorly from the customary functional dissociation in which my spiritually awakened self and my traumatized self could get along in ways that allowed me to function and live my life. But now my dissociative self was not strong enough to hold back the traumatizing feelings that came rolling out with great force, bringing me down into truly scary and disoriented places from which I could not shake loose.

In some strange way this fragmented state of mind felt like the sheep barn experience in reverse. For in the sheep barn experience I was carried away by God beyond my experience of myself in ego consciousness into heaven. But now in the depths of my traumatized and traumatizing fears it felt as if I were being carried away into realms beyond my manageable experience of myself in ego consciousness into the outer fringes of hell. Someone once told me in spiritual direction that "there is a place where the depths of God, the depths of hell and the depths of self are one." That captures something of the enigmatic state in which I found myself.

This unfolding drama with the priest occurred in the middle of winter, when my duties at the pig barn included watching over a boar and herd of sows in a fenced-off wooded area on the monastery grounds. One day, during a particularly bitter spell of cold weather, the boar walked onto the ice of a small pond in those woods. Under his immense weight he fell through the ice and drowned. With this imagery in my mind, I began to experience my sanity as thin ice over bitterly cold water. I sensed that the thin ice was beginning to break apart, causing me to fall into the icy depths of a psychotic break from which, given my history of trauma and fragility, I might never return.

It was then that I knew what I must do. I wrote to my mother, telling her that I was leaving the monastery and asking her if my father would let me come home. In her letter back she said that my father said he would be willing to let me come back home.

The next time I went to confession I told the priest that I had suddenly decided that I needed to leave the monastery to go home to confront my father about the damaging effects of his abuse of me as a child. But I did not mention anything to the priest about the role he played in precipitating the crisis that required my urgent need to leave the monastery, for I feared that doing so would hurt his feelings.

I wrote a letter to the abbot telling him that for reasons I did not want to discuss I wanted to leave the monastery immediately and return to my home in Akron, Ohio. When I dropped my letter into the slot in his office door, I knew there was no turning back.

I timed the delivery of that letter so that I could go straight to my scheduled session of spiritual direction with Father John Eudes, who was in charge of the monks such as myself who had made their temporary vows. I began my session with Father John Eudes by telling him that, for personal reasons I did not want to discuss, I needed to leave the monastery immediately. He was very surprised about what I was saying, and he asked if I would be willing to discuss with him what had led me to this decision. I told him no, that my mind was settled, that I needed to leave immediately. He said, fine, that he would talk to the abbot, and I would be getting instructions about when and how I would be leaving.

I walked out of his office in the infirmary and into the small infirmary chapel where I knelt on the floor near the entrance. Through the window of the chapel I could see the sheep barn. An old lay brother was sitting off to the side, where he had fallen asleep while praying with his rosary wrapped around his hand. I had so wanted and never questioned that I would be spending my life here, giving my life to God in prayerful silence. I had so wanted and never questioned that I would die here and be buried with the monks who had died and crossed over before me into God, just as monks have died and crossed over into God down through the centuries. But now none of that was going to happen. Now for me there was only a future that seemed to be no future at all with nowhere to go except back to my life in the world I had left behind when I came to the monastery. And kneeling there in that sense of utter loss, I started to cry.

I burned my journals and my poetry, but I did keep and bring with me my handwritten philosophy exams. I got permission to talk to Thomas Merton, who was at this point living in his hermitage. I did not tell Merton that my confessor, whom he so admired, was at the heart of my decision to leave. I simply told Merton that I needed to go home to confront my father about how he had abused me as a child. Because of my ongoing commitment to spending time alone in the sheep barn and my interest in receiving his guidance in reading the classical texts of the mystics, Merton thought I had a vocation to solitude. He gave me the address of a Benedictine monk who might accept me as a member of a small group of hermits that he had gathered about him in Nova Scotia.

I had always wondered how people left the monastery. Someone who had always been at his place in the refectory and the choir was suddenly gone, but because we never spoke to each other, we never knew the details of his departure. I was told that on Sunday when the community and the retreatants were all at Mass I was to go to a certain room in the guesthouse. In that room I found a pair of blue jeans, several shirts, along with my high school book bag and the clothes I had brought with me when I entered the monastery, as well as an envelope that contained, if I remember correctly, a thousand dollars and a plane ticket.

I took off my monastic habit and put on the secular clothes that felt strangely familiar to me. I walked alone through the empty hallways of the guesthouse and out through the gates of the monastery, past the words "God Alone" carved in stone at the entrance and on to the avenue of trees, where a driver was waiting to drive me to the Louisville airport. As I flew home, it seemed that I was flying into a void without any meaningful or foreseeable future.

Please notice that I left the monastery in very much the same way that I left my home to enter the monastery. By that I mean, just as I left home without being able to find the courage to confront my father, in very much same way I left the monastery without being able to find the courage to confront the priest or to report what he had done to me to Thomas Merton, Father John Eudes, or the abbot.

As you will see in the chapters yet to come, it was going to be almost another twenty years before I would be healed from my longstanding fear of being true to myself in the midst of my own life. I had no way of knowing when I left the monastery that my healing path would bring me through so many more transformations, on up to who I now know and experience myself to be as I share my journey with you in these reflections.

May each of us learn in moments when everything seems lost that our unknown tomorrows will bring yet

more perils from which will arise yet more unforeseeable blessings. And that our providential journey
through all these experiences is an ongoing dress re-
hearsal for our approaching death, in which our utter
demise will open out upon our eternal fulfillment and
liberation.

Amen. So be it.

8

The Long Way Home

The abrupt transition from having lived nearly six
years in the cloistered silence of the monastery
to being back in the world I had left behind was, at
first, too much for me to process in any coherent and
meaningful way. What added to the struggle was that
I still found it hard to believe I was no longer in the
monastery and that the sequence of events leading up
to my need to leave had actually happened.

What was both unsettling and meaningful in my
first few weeks at home was that my mother put me in
the same bedroom that I had slept in during my four
years of high school. Everything in that room seemed
so strangely familiar: the same faded blue wool carpet,
the same bed in the same corner of the room, and,
looking out the window, the same view of the long
hedgerow that lined the front of the yard. It was the

same hedgerow my father was trimming when I told him about my plan to enter the monastery, and he told me that if I went there, he would kill my mother to punish me.

As I drifted off to sleep in those first nights sleeping in that room, I could see myself in my mind's eye when I was in high school, kneeling there on the floor in the darkness, illumined by the blue glass vigil light that burned before the statue of Mary and the pictures of Jesus and the saints. I could interiorly see and feel myself as I was back then, kneeling with my rosary wrapped around my hand, bowing over, touching my forehead to the floor, asking God to have mercy on me and to sustain me in the traumatizing fear that I lived in day by day. And I could remember—no, not just remember, but relive within myself the mysterious ways that God's presence had flowed so sweetly and so subtly into hidden depths within myself, letting me know I was not alone in the midst of my overwhelming feelings of sadness and fear.

I remembered, too, how I used to drift off to sleep in that very bed in which I was now sleeping, holding fast within my heart the words that I was reading each day in Thomas Merton's journal, *The Sign of Jonas*, in which he said so many deep and beautiful things about the intimate nearness of God that he experienced in his silent life of prayer in the monastery.

And I remembered that fateful night when I rose from that bed and fled in my exodus to that far-off place of silence and prayer, where I was graced with inner quickenings in the loft of the abandoned sheep barn or sitting in the snow at the base of a tree as God walked by and looked at me, as if in a dream, through the eyes of a passing deer. And I remembered the place where, in so many other ways as well, I was touched by deepening realizations of God's presence in my life. And I remembered how grateful I felt to live in the community of men who, like me, had come there to seek and find and give themselves to God in the hidden life of silence and prayer.

And I painfully remembered how one of those men in his brokenness made a move on me. And how I, in my brokenness, passively yielded to his ways, leading me little by little to the brink of losing my mind, sending me in a state near panic back out here into the world I had left behind. It seemed then that in returning home my life had come full circle. Only now my situation was much worse than it was when I was in high school. For now, there was no holy place I could flee to find refuge in God beyond the sadness and uncertainties that now stirred anew in the broken places in my mind and heart.

What added to my feelings of loss and confusion was that in returning home I no longer felt at home in my own Catholic faith, which had been my spiritual home since I was a small child. Coming fresh from my downfall in the monastery I would go to Mass on Sunday with my mother and grandmother and find myself sitting there, unable to see how God could buy into an outfit like this. The whole Catholic thing seemed to me at the time to be so hypocritical, so driven by an all-male clergy invested with spiritual authority, regardless of the extent to which they may really have been grounded in humility and true to the imperatives of Christlike love for those they served.

It was in the midst of these interior upheavals and loss of spiritual rootedness that I found solace and a sense of security in falling back into the deeply dissociative states that allowed me as a child to survive the ongoing trauma that seemed to threaten my very existence.

As it turned out, I was going to live in that emotionally disconnected way for a number of years yet to come. I would not say that I was emotionally numb during those years. It seems truer to say that I was extremely guarded and protective in seeing to it that no one could get close enough to me that I would have to risk painful encounters that might ignite the intense emotions of betrayal, fear, and confusion that were hidden away inside of me.

It was in that dissociative, disconnected survival strategy that I began to make decisions that perpetuated the painful and chaotic patterns of my childhood and adolescence. The first and most far-reaching of these early dysfunctional decisions was that I asked the first woman I had ever dated and whom I had known for only for a couple of months to marry me. And she, in her own emotional immaturity, said yes. We eloped to Monroe, Michigan, where we were married by a justice of the peace and returned to Akron, where we lived in the attic of my parents' home. From the very beginning of our marriage a pattern emerged in which our feelings of love for each other were repeatedly compromised by ongoing arguments that never really got resolved.

By the time my wife and I had been married for several years, we were living in a mobile home with our daughter, who was just learning to walk and who was going to be joined a bit later by our second daughter. I was attending classes at the University of Akron, majoring in English literature and education, and teaching sixth grade in a nearby Catholic school on a temporary certificate provided by the Cleveland diocese.

It was during this time that I began to realize how lost I felt in my own life. My wife and I seemed gridlocked in argumentative patterns in which my emotionally distancing ways triggered her feelings of emotional abandonment and anger toward me. This, in turn, triggered my childhood fears of being threatened by my father's anger. Round and round we went in patterns of fear, anger, and resentment that we could not understand. Nor did we know how to reach out for the help that might have rescued the slowly sinking ship of our marriage.

It was in the midst of these unsettling patterns of ongoing marital strife that I began to realize that what I wanted more than anything else was to be grounded once again in the experience of the communal presence with God that had so transformed my life since I was small child, and which had deepened all the more in the monastery. By communal presence with God, I mean that unitive experience of accessing and being accessed by God in ways in which God and I mutually disappeared as dualistically other than each other. By communal presence with God, I mean that state of sustained awareness infused with love in which I intimately realized that my very presence embodied the presence of God in my nothingness without God. By communal presence with God, I mean the ways in which I would sit in the loft of the abandoned sheep barn, given over to the divinity of barn swallows swooping this way and that over the meadow and the smell of the freshly plowed fields after a rain, all this woven, along with the trees and stars, into an all-pervasive unitive mystery that alone is ultimately real.

I could not at first see how it was possible for me to fulfill these reawakened longings. For, whereas every aspect of monastic life was carefully crafted to nurture the contemplative way of life in which the communal presence of God is realized, every aspect of the fast-moving ways of the world seemed to be moving in the opposite direction. Then it dawned on me that the contemplative way of life is not dependent on the monastic life that nurtures and protects it. My capacity to live a contemplative way of life was inscribed in my very being as a person created in the image and likeness of God. And so I came to the graced realization that I could, in the midst of my life in the world, cultivate a contemplative culture in my heart by renewing my fidelity to a daily quiet time in which I could once again learn from God how to love and be loved by God.

And so I began to get up early each morning as my wife and young daughter were still asleep. I would light a candle and sit out on the floor in the living room in an interior stance of silence and openness to God. I did not expect God to show up right away, for I had been away for a while and my heart needed to relearn how to enter into that interior stance of heartfelt attentiveness in which the presence of God begins to make itself known.

I was keenly aware of the risks of launching off on my own in my search for God without the trustworthy guidance and nurturance of contemplative Christianity in which I was immersed in the monastery. It was not that I doubted that God was still there for me in the interior resources of my Catholic faith, but rather that I could not turn to those sources without betraying my own heart, which was still so wounded by what had happened to me in the monastery.

It was at this point in my healing journey that I began to reflect on how graced I was in the monastery by the non-Christian spiritual masters who came to Gethsemani to visit Merton: the Vietnamese Buddhist monk Thich Nhat Hanh; the Jewish mystic and philosopher Abraham Joshua Heschel; the Muslim Sufis; the Hindu yogi who had come from India to found an ashram; Bede Griffiths, the Benedictine monk who was living as a Christian yogi in his ashram in India; and John Wu, a Chinese Catholic who, in his visit with Merton, spoke to us of the rich resonance he saw between the Chinese Taoist tradition and the contemplative foundations of the Gospel. In his translation of the Gospels into Chinese he translated the opening words of the Gospel of John, "In the beginning was the Word and the Word was with God," as "In the beginning was the Tao and the Tao was with God."

With Merton's help I came to realize that God's presence is fanned out into these contemplative traditions of the world's great religions as so many languages or paths to contemplative communion with the divine mystery that he and I were seeking in our own Christian tradition. And I recalled how I, with Merton's help, began my first feeble attempts to read the classical texts of the non-Christian traditions with the same devotional sincerity with which I read the Gospels and the mystic teachers of my own Christian tradition.

And so, when I got up each morning to meditate as my wife and young daughter slept, I began to renew my prayerful study of the classical texts of these non-Christian sources of contemplative wisdom. I renewed my practice of yoga, which I had discovered through Thomas Merton, along with what I learned from him about the Buddhist traditions of meditation as a path to ultimate liberation.

In a way that seemed quite natural to me, I began again to read the writings of Thomas Merton as a spiritual master in my own Christian tradition with the same interior openness that I was reading the non-Christian spiritual masters. As I read passages in Merton's writings and quietly whispered his words to myself as I read, I was surprised and delighted to hear myself whispering words of contemplative wisdom in the mother tongue of my own Christian tradition. It was in this way that Thomas Merton once again became my spiritual guide, leading me back, without resistance, into a contemplative understanding of the Bible and a heartfelt reunion with the deathless presence of Jesus, who had been patiently waiting for me during my self-imposed exile from the spiritual home of my own Catholic tradition. What

added to my renewed bond with Merton as my teacher is
that it was at this time I was contacted by the monastery,
letting me know that Thomas Merton had died in his
travels to Bangkok, Thailand.

I am now going to move ahead another seven years
in my healing journey. I had at this point recently left
classroom teaching to be on the pastoral team of a large
parish in Rocky River, a suburb on the west side of
Cleveland, Ohio, where I served as director of religious
education. My wife and I continued on as before with
our sincere feelings of love for each other repeatedly
compromised by unresolved feelings of anger and fear.
What was especially unfortunate was that our two
daughters, now ages seven and four, were burdened by
our inability as their parents to provide them with the
emotional stability and nurturing support that children
need and deserve.

It was in the midst of these turbulent emotional patterns that I felt called to write a book on Thomas Merton. For the next few years I rose early each morning
to sit alone in silence, prayerfully absorbed in passages
in Merton's writings that invite us to understand the
spiritual life as the transformative journey of learning
how to join God in knowing who God knows and
calls us to be. My solitary absorption in the depth and
beauty of those passages often silenced me into states of
prayerfully resting in God resting in me, in ways beyond
what words can say.

And from the hidden depths of that communal silence, words flowed into my conscious awareness, and I would write them down, feeling very much like a faithful scribe taking dictation. I would then rewrite and rewrite and rewrite those words, being careful not to meddle with the raw purity of poetic phrases, while at the same time trying to clear away the dross of my wordy inadequacies.

The transformative graces given to me in the hours I spent writing in this way consisted of honoring the first stirrings of a barely discernible desire to pass on to others intimate matters of the spirit that had been and were currently being passed on to me. It felt safe to be so bold as to attempt such an offering because I knew my reflections might never be published. And, at the same time, I felt and believed that our heartfelt desires to share intimate matters of the spirit in ways that may never be seen or heard or understood by anyone are heard and seen and carried forth in God, touching the world in ways that I did not need to understand.

When the book was finished, I titled it *Merton's Palace of Nowhere,* a phrase taken from Merton's rendering of the words of the Taoist sage Chuang Tzu: "Come with me to the palace of nowhere where all the many things are one."[1] When Ave Maria Press published

---

[1] Thomas Merton, *The Way of Chuang Tzu* (New York: New Directions, 1965), 123–24.

my book in 1979, I began to accept invitations to lead weekend contemplative retreats at Catholic retreat houses in the United States and Canada. When I began to prepare to lead these retreats, I wrote to Dan Walsh, who had taught me medieval philosophy at the monastery, asking for any suggestions he might have that would help me communicate to the retreatants in ways that would awaken them to their ultimate identity, subsisting in God as light subsists in flame.

He responded, telling me that I could not communicate this unitive mystery, but it would communicate itself through me if I was convinced about what I said and if I truly was what I said. And he told me that I would know the unitive mystery was communicating itself because there would be a response in the listeners in which deep calls unto deep, allowing the listeners to know that something very deep within themselves that mattered very much was being addressed.

I was blessed in speaking to the retreatants in this intimate language of awakening. I was blessed twice over at the end of each conference when I would ask if there were any questions or if there was anything anyone felt moved to share. And as someone raised their hand and began to speak, my own awakened heart could sense when their words were flowing, unfiltered from the depths of their own awakening heart.

If, as was often the case, this movement into these interior realms of the spirit was new to those who raised their hand. I sensed they were not able consciously to appreciate and understand the far-reaching implications of the intimations of God's oneness with them that were flowing through them as they spoke. This was because it is only in learning to be faithful to a daily rendezvous with God in meditation and prayer that the reflective mind learns consciously to discern and to yield to God's oneness with us in our longings for deeper union with God, who is the origin and fulfillment of our longings. (This is especially so for the vast majority of us who are seeking deeper union with God in the midst of the world's often stressful and distracting ways.)

As for those present who had been traveling this interior path for quite some time, I sensed in their questions and sharings that they were already in the midst of learning not to be surprised by the setbacks intermingled with the graced breakthroughs that occur on this healing path. On the path to eternal fulfillment, which never ends, we all die as beginners.

As I sit here writing, I wonder if these words are but the idle musings of an old man. Possibly. But my own awakening heart tells me that thoughts such as the ones I am sharing with you here embody intimations of the deathless nature of ourselves that flow on and on in the eternality of each passing moment of our lives. I say *our* lives instead of simply my life because it is my intention as well as my hope that by sharing these interior dimensions of myself I will help you to access the ways in which you, much like those attending my silent retreats, are being interiorly drawn to follow the promptings of your own awakening heart.

I end this chapter with the prayerful hope that each of us, at our own pace and in our own unique way, will continue to realize that:

Finding our way along the healing path does not consist of striving for some far-off goal that we may or may not attain, but is rather a way of a discovering a secret hidden deep within our hearts.

Finding our way along the healing path does not consist of figuring out some obscure teaching but rather consists of learning to see God hidden and revealed in all that we see.

Finding our way along the healing path does not consist of mastering some method of meditation but rather consists of learning not to do violence to the fragility of our waiting.

Amen. So be it.

9

The Healing Journey
in Traumatizing Time

One of the first invitations I received to lead a weekend contemplative retreat came from a clinical psychologist named John Finch, who invited me to lead a retreat that he offered each year in Seattle, Washington, for his patients, former patients, and other mental-health professionals. At the end of the retreat he made me an unexpected and life-changing offer. He told me that he wanted me to consider accepting a scholarship with family support to be a full-time student in the five-year doctoral program in clinical psychology at the Graduate School of Psychology at Fuller Theological Seminary in Pasadena, California.

Surprised and trying to take in what he was saying, I told him that I did not have the grade point average that would qualify me to be accepted into a doctoral program. He told me that in this program at Fuller each tenured professor in the doctoral program could choose one student who would automatically be accepted into the program on the condition that the student passed all the exams and met the other requirements of the doctoral program. He told me that a tenured professor at the graduate school was attending the retreat I had just given and that, after listening to my talks, he told John Finch that he would accept me as his special student. Beyond the other requirements, he added that at the heart of his offer was that I would commit myself to developing an academic model that would support and shed light on the contribution that the contemplative traditions make to mental health. He told me to go home, talk it over with my wife, and let him know my decision.

To make a long story short, I accepted his offer to move with my wife and two children from our home in the Midwest to Pasadena, California, to begin a five-year commitment to full-time doctoral studies in clinical psychology. I clearly recall feeling that what was happening was so strangely similar to my experience of reading Thomas Merton in high school, which led me, within days after graduating, to get up in the middle of the night, leave my home in Akron, Ohio, and enter the monastery. In both instances I was heading off into uncharted waters, which, I felt in my heart, I was being called to explore.

In accepting this opportunity, my gratitude was mingled with stress at the thought of keeping up with my studies while at the same time continuing to lead contemplative weekend retreats almost every other weekend in the United States and Canada.

What added to the ongoing stress was that by my third year into the program, I knew I had done little to deserve the trust placed in me to demonstrate the contribution that the contemplative traditions can make to the field of mental health. It was not that I had not brought with me into the doctoral program insights into contemplative dimensions of healing, but rather that I was not able to find a way to express my insights in a manner that could be helpful to clinicians and those in therapy.

By now I had come to the point in my doctoral program in which I was to begin a year of training as a psychological intern at a Veterans Administration hospital. In one of my rotations at this hospital I was assigned to an inpatient alcohol treatment unit. The men on this unit were mostly Vietnam vets, many of whom would meet the criteria for the dual diagnosis of post-traumatic stress disorder and alcohol abuse and dependency. They knew firsthand how the traumas they endured on the battlefield continued to wage on within them as nightmares, flashbacks of traumatizing experiences, and other psychological symptoms of post-traumatic stress disorder. They knew firsthand how their attempts to self-medicate their symptoms with alcohol had created another life-threatening battle within themselves that made the severity of their symptoms worse. And they knew firsthand that their finite and wounded powers were powerless to break free from the forces of addiction that were on the way to destroying their lives.

On the morning that I arrived for the first time on the addiction recovery unit I was told that some years earlier the men on the unit had devised an initiation rite for those seeking to be admitted to the unit. Because this initiation rite had been handed down as a secret oral tradition, I myself did not know anything about what I was about to witness.

What struck me when I entered the room where the initiation rite was to occur was that all the men on the unit were sitting in chairs lining the four walls of the room, leaving the large area in the middle of the room empty, except for two chairs facing each other about four feet apart. The arrangement of chairs around the empty space reminded me of a Zen meditation hall. All the men on the unit were sitting there in silence, waiting for the newcomer to be brought in.

When the person seeking to be admitted to the unit was led into the room, he was instructed to sit on one of the two chairs in the middle of the room. One of the men in the unit, a recovering alcoholic who was conducting the initiation rite, sat on the other chair facing the newcomer. All the men sitting around the four walls room sat in silence, looking downward with no eye contact, no smiles, creating a somber atmosphere as serious as death, befitting the situation of the newcomer, who was at risk of dying from the effects of his addiction.

It was in this communal silence that the person leading the initiation rite asked the newcomer, "What do you love the most?" Not knowing just what to say, the person said, "My wife." At which point, everyone seated around the four walls of the room yelled as loud as they could, "BULLSHIT." The man being questioned nearly leapt out of his seat in being startled by the piercing yell. Then everyone looked back down to the floor in somber-faced silence.

The person was again asked, "What do you love the most?" This time the man, with some trepidation, said, "My children." At which point all the men yelled, "BULLSHIT," followed again by somber-faced silence. The same question was repeated with the same results until finally the man said, "Alcohol." The moment the person said "alcohol," everyone stood and gave him a standing ovation. He was asked to stand. Then, in complete silence, they all lined up single file as each man embraced the newcomer into their midst.

As the man was being briefly held by each person, tears began to stream down his face. I sensed within myself that this was possibly the first time this man had been touched, really touched, in a long, long time, maybe ever. My own eyes filled up with tears as I was drawn into the healing energies of this event. And within myself I heard the voice that interiorly speaks to me at such times say, "This is just like at the monastery!" Right at that moment it was clear to me that the deep healing that was stirring in this place in these people was continuous with the deep healing of contemplative living that monastic life is intended to invite and sustain.

That very day, driving home from the VA hospital, I knew what I was to do. I was to interiorly turn to the man as he stood there with tears streaming down his face as my mentor. For by attempting to put words to the graced awakening in which he was being transformed in that life-changing moment, I would be putting words to the contribution that the contemplative traditions make to mental health.

The qualities that I will now share with you began to emerge one by one in my understanding of this man's experience. I came to realize that *in his moment of awakening, he was vulnerable. And in his vulnerability, true invincibility was being manifested in the world.*

Thomas Merton wrote that in the depths of our true self where we are one with God we are not subject to the brutalities of our own will.[1] No matter how badly we may have trashed ourselves in patterns of self-destructive behavior that ritualistically reenact the traumatizing ways we were treated, this innermost hidden center of ourselves remains invincibly whole and undiminished because it is that part of us that belongs entirely to God.

I came to realize that as the man stood there with tears streaming down his face. *he was childlike*, meaning he was guileless and open-faced, free of posing and posturing. And in his childlike transparency, true spiritual maturity was being manifested in the world. Such are those who are simply present in sincere, earthy, transparent, and loving ways that are free of pretense and calculating strategies as to how to leverage the situation to serve their private whims and desires.

As the man stood there in his moment of self-disclosure, *he was alone. He was unto himself.* And in that moment he bore witness to the unitive mystery in which, as the psychologist D. Winnicott expressed it,

---

[1] Thomas Merton, *Conjectures of a Guilty Bystander* (New York: Doubleday, 1966), 142.

We are all *alone together.* Once, in the monastery, Merton was speaking to the novices about an elderly monk who had just died. I can remember Merton saying that in the hour of your death you can get all the people in the room with you that you want to. They can climb up into the bed with you if you want. But you are dying alone. And you are that alone right now. You will never find true and abiding intimacy running from that solitary aloneness, but only by entering into that solitude in which God's abyss-like intimacy with you, with all of us, and with all things lies hidden.

As the man stood there being embraced by one recovering alcoholic after another, *he knew nothing. In this unknowing, all his foggy assumptions, conclusions, and answers that were formed and sustained in his addiction were eclipsed by a luminous, empty-handed understanding that lit up his mind and heart in ways that he had not as yet even begun to comprehend.*

The sixteenth-century Spanish mystic Saint John of the Cross says that "God grants to some people an experience of God that is so lofty that they understand clearly that everything remains to be understood."[2] In the twelve-step tradition of recovery there is the "Set Aside

---

[2] "The Spiritual Canticle," stanza 7, *The Collected Works of Saint John of the Cross,* rev. ed., ed. Kieran Kavanaugh and Otilio Rodriguez (Washington, DC: Institute of Carmelite Studies, 1971), 502.

Prayer," in which the addict asks his or her higher power to "help me to set aside everything I think I know."

Standing in the unseen light of the awakening moment, we begin to discover a deeper way to understand what it means to understand. At the level of ego-functioning, to understand means to comprehend an idea or set of ideas. But here, in the vertical, depth dimension of the hidden foundations of inner liberation, to understand means to realize in some unexplainable way one's immersion in a fullness of Presence that cannot be explained.

In the moment of his awakening, *he was silent, in being silenced by the numinous Presence that transcends what words can say.* Just as we are silenced in those moments we are graced with a fleeting glimpse of the fullness of presence that is accessing us and taking us to itself in ways we cannot and do not need to explain. This, it seems to me, is where solitude and silence are so at home with each other. For in our moments of awakening we cannot explain to anybody, including ourselves, what is happening to us.

And this, it seems to me, is where we can distinguish two very different kinds of words. There are words that disturb the quiet clarity by attempting to explain what cannot be explained. And there are words that resonate, embody, and bear witness to a unitive experience in the midst of which we realize ourselves to be so grateful and amazed. Such are the words of lovers and poets.

Such are the words of philosophers who bear witness to the mystery of being. Such are the words of scripture, contemplatively understood. And such are the words of saints and mystics down through the ages. Such was the word *alcohol* and all words that come from those who admit what they are afraid to admit, which is the very thing they need to admit to be set free. And, I hope, such are the words I am sharing with you in these reflections.

And I was able to realize that, as the alcoholic stood there with tears streaming down his face, *he was dying before our very eyes. For in this moment the alcoholic in him that, for so many years claimed to have the final say in who he was, was dying. And in this death he was being born before our very eyes as someone newly emerging out of the darkness into the light.* The room in which his awakening occurred seemed to me to be at once a hospice and a maternity ward. For the room embodied the intimately realized mystery of life out of death.

As I reflected on all this, it was clear to me that *this man's moment of deliverance was not the end of a journey but the beginning of a much longer one.* For the habits of mind and heart formed in trauma, abandonment, and addiction are very strong. It was true that in the graced moment I have just described, he was a momentary mystic, momentarily set free from the tyranny of his suffering. But it was also true that he was not going to be able to live in an abiding awareness of the depths so fleetingly glimpsed, for the simple reason that he was an alcoholic. But the fleeting taste of realized freedom and liberation could become for him a light that illuminated the path, the way of life that sustained and deepened in his ongoing willingness to hand his life over to the care of the higher power that had accessed him and set his heart alight as he stood there with tears streaming down his face.

As I turned my attention to the men coming up one by one to hold him, it seemed to me at first that they were welcoming him in their midst. And while this was certainly true, I also sensed that as each of them was embracing him, they longed to get a dose of the golden glow of deliverance that was flowing fresh from the opening, in which, day by day, their own lives were being sustained and transformed.

I came away from the healing event that I was privileged to experience at the VA hospital with a more refined understanding of the healing energies that are released in moments of spiritual awakening. I realized that to understand this transformative process from the vantage point of religious faith was to realize in these moments of awakening the presence of God. That presence causes our soul, which is to say, the interiority of ourselves, to glow with the qualities of God. In the light of this glowing, our soul, like the wick of a burning candle, shines brightly with the qualities of God, instilled in us by God as persons made in the image and likeness of God.

So it is that we, in the graced moments of our awakening, are rendered utterly vulnerable in realizing we are powerless to diminish how invincibly precious we are in God's eyes in the midst of our wayward ways. So it is that we, in our graced moments of awakening, are momentarily silenced in realizing ourselves to be ineffably absorbed in the presence of God, beyond what words can say. And so on with the litany of the Godly qualities and blessings instilled in us by God in creating us in the image and likeness of God.

As we have seen in the previous chapters of this book, these graced awakenings sometimes occur in moments that are inherently endowed with a sense of well-being and fulfillment. While out walking in the midst of nature, we, in turning to see a flock of birds descending, might glimpse, as if out of the corner of our eye, something of the birds' descent that is primordial, vast, and ultimately divine. Or in surrendering ourselves to the beloved's sweet embrace, or in looking down into a child's upturned face, or in something as simple as a quiet hour alone at day's end, there can flash forth that fleeting glimpse of God's oneness with us in the intimate immediacy of life itself.

And we have seen that these interior quickenings sometimes occur in traumatizing times. That is how I was initiated into the realm of blessedness when God merged with me as a small child lying alone in the dark, filled with fear and sadness. And so, too, with the divinizing moment in which the man in the midst of his initiation rite admitted "alcohol," thereby evoking his graced awakening.

And so it seems to me that just as alchemists of old devoted themselves to turning lead into gold, we, who have been blessed to have been drawn out onto the healing path, are discovering within ourselves that the polar opposite realms of traumatizing bitterness and tender sweetness are themselves permeated with the graced alchemy of a sustaining Presence that utterly transcends, even as it utterly permeates, the vicissitudes of all that life might send our way. And this intimately realized alchemy lets us know, from somewhere deep within, how important it is to be courageously gentle with ourselves as we experience how moments of sweetness we do not want to pass away keep passing away, just as moments of sorrow and loss we wish would never occur, continue to occur.

As we learn to settle into an underlying, habitual understanding of this graced alchemy, a kind of quiet confidence can begin to grow within us in knowing that God, who has begun this work in us, will bring it to completion up to and including the moment of our death and beyond.

Because my explorations have brought me to the graced awakenings that can occur in death it seems fitting to bring this chapter to a close by sharing a healing experience that graced my life in my rotation at the VA hospital working with terminal patients. In the unit to which I was assigned there were four men in the final stages of chronic obstructive pulmonary disease, in which death occurs as the lungs become increasingly incapable of absorbing oxygen. My task as a psychological intern was to go in and talk to each of the four men on the unit, assessing, charting, and, hopefully, helping with depression or other psychological factors relative to their overall level of functioning.

Three of the men on the unit were quite willing to talk to me. In reading the chart of the fourth man, who had just arrived on the unit, I saw that he was reported as being an angry, divorced, chain-smoking, alcoholic businessman. He was uncooperative with his treatment regimen, and he had told the other three men on the unit that he did not want to communicate with them in any way. When I introduced myself, he told me that he did not want to talk to me, either. I explained to him that I was required to talk to him because I had to record that I had done so in his chart but that I would honor his request by keeping my time with him very brief.

In one of our brief encounters he opened his pajama top and said, "Look at this muscle spasm on my ribs." I later went in to see him the day he got the results of the biopsy that revealed that what he thought was a muscle spasm was an aggressive cancer coming out through his chest wall. When I approached his bed, he reached out to take my hand, and as he held my hand he said, "I wasn't born a son of a bitch, I became one. I think I'm going to give it up." I said, "You mean you're going to retire from being a son of a bitch?" He said, "I am." And he did. From that day forward he cooperated with his treatment regimen. He was friendly with the other three men on the unit. I talked to his adult son out in the hallway, who told me, with tears in his eyes, that this was the first time his father had ever really talked to him.

When I went into the room a few days after he had died, I talked with the other three men who were still there, lying in their beds, wearing their oxygen masks. We all agreed what a good man he was and how grateful we were to get to know him. Sometimes, in the eleventh hour we can save our life, and, in the process, bless those fortunate enough to be with us in the hour of our deliverance. Of course, there are those who die with no outward signs of being interiorly set free from the tyranny of death. For them our faith tells us that their graced and eternal awakening occurs in realms of light beyond the darkness of this world.

Over the years Maureen would write spiritual sayings on pieces of paper that I keep finding tucked away, here and there. Just this past week I came across one of her handwritten sayings by Ram Dass that reads, "Death is safe. It is like taking off a tight shoe at the end of the day." I am now recalling how I shared in the introduction of this book my experience of sitting next to Maureen as she was dying. And I recall that as I gazed into the surrendered serenity of her face, I knew that I was gazing into the gate of heaven.

May each of us at our own pace and in our own way continue to find our way along this path, this way of life, in which we are learning from Love how to be healed from habits of our minds and hearts that compromise and do violence to Love. And may we continue on in this way, through all our days, learning from Love how to die of Love until in the end there will be nothing left of us but Love. And may we, within ourselves, know and trust that when the moment of our death finally comes, that nothing will happen, save being transported from a veiled to an unveiled immersion in the deathless mystery of Love that has been welling up and giving itself to us in and as each passing moment of our lives.

Amen. So be it.

10

The Gift

As I was nearing the end of my doctoral studies, the longstanding difficulties my wife and I were having in feeling loved, accepted, and understood by each other continued to intensify. Then, on Christmas Eve of my final year of my studies, our marriage began to dramatically unravel. The precipitating event occurred as my wife and I and our two daughters were decorating the Christmas tree when our oldest daughter, who had graduated from high school the year earlier, nervously announced that she was pregnant. In telling you how my wife and I responded to her pregnancy, I feel that I am letting you in on the ways my first wife and I were at our worst. And there is some truth to that. But at a more interior level that concerns us here, it is truer to say that I will be sharing the ways we were the most broken, and how we each acted out our brokenness on ourselves, on each other, and on our children.

When I say we, I am not simply referring to my wife and myself, for I have in mind all the ways that we as human beings fall into patterns of hurting ourselves as well as the very people we intended and hoped to love and to be loved by in return. More significantly still, I am seeking here to bear witness to the mystery of experiential salvation in which the depths of spiritual healing can emerge out of the depths of our brokenness, when our brokenness is deeply seen and deeply accepted.

I have no memory of the firestorm of intense emotions that immediately followed our daughter's announcement, except for the singular moment when my wife, while pointing at her, screamed at me, "I want her out of this house!"

As terrible as that was, I did something just as terrible. In my passivity and fear of my wife's anger, I drove my daughter to Saint Ann's Home, a church-run residence for unwed mothers. As I drove my daughter to the facility, I tried to reassure her, telling her that we were just going to look at the place, to check it out. But she just sat there, looking straight ahead, saying nothing.

When we arrived at the facility, the nun who was leading us on a guided tour paused at the open door of one of the small bedrooms that lined a long hallway. As we looked into one of the rooms with its two beds, a sink, and a table, she told my daughter that if she decided to stay there that she would be staying in one of these rooms with another young woman until her child was born.

It was at that point that I suddenly realized at the feeling level what was happening. I thanked the nun for the tour and told her I would be in touch with her about our decision. But as soon as my daughter and I got in the car, I told her that she was not going to have to go to that place. She was going to stay home where she belonged. Again, I must say I have no memory of the intense interactions that occurred between my wife and myself when I told her I was not going to comply with her demands that our daughter be sent away. But what I do remember is that in the heat of the moment I took all my clothes out of our bedroom and piled them up in the family room where, from that point on, I slept on the sofa.

In the days that followed I did another terrible thing with respect to being the father my daughter needed me to be. I told her that she needed to take responsibility for what she had done. And for that reason, I would not be providing financial help in any way in raising her child! I did this knowing she had no money and so had no way of caring for her own child, my own grandchild. Not only did I feel fine about doing this, but what is more, I believed it was my responsibility as her father and as a practicing Catholic to teach her to take responsibility for the consequences of her behavior.

I vaguely remember a conversation in which I told my daughter that I did not believe in abortion, but if she wanted to terminate her pregnancy, I would support her in doing that. She told me that she wanted to have her child. And that began for us a search in which we discovered a program in Tustin, California, south of where we lived, in which the birth mother could choose the adoptive parents of her child. As part of the agreement the adoptive parents would send photos and details of the child growing up. When the adoptive parents felt the child was ready, they could, at their own discretion, begin to gently introduce the child, step by step, to the situation. And, if the adoptive parents and the child agreed, the child could meet his or her birth mother to see if they might have an ongoing relationship while the child continued living with his or her adoptive parents.

My daughter and I both liked this program. My daughter looked through a book in which couples presented their photos and expressed why they wanted to adopt a child. My daughter chose a married couple that she really liked. The husband was a psychiatrist, and his wife was an artist. In reading how they described themselves and their marriage and their love for their own children, they seemed to my daughter to be a mature couple who would provide a loving home to her child.

A requirement for being admitted into this program was that the birth mother and her family had to have one session with a staff member of the program who was a clinical psychologist. My wife and I and our two daughters were uneasy in going into this session in which we had no way of knowing what to expect.

The therapist began by asking, "If dreams came true and there was something at home that would make your life happier, what would that be?" My youngest daughter volunteered to go first, saying that she would like it if her mother and older sister did not fight so much. At that point my wife stood up and said, "I can tell I am about to get gangbanged," and walked out of the room. In a calm, clear voice the therapist asked my two daughters, "If this had happened at home, what would happen next?" They both said, "Our father would tell us not to upset our mother and go find her to try to calm her down." The therapist asked them, "And how do you feel when your father does that?" They both said, in an emotionally decisive way, that they did not like it when I did that.

As the three of us walked out of the office at the end of the session, we discovered that my wife had driven off, leaving us there in the parking lot. Sometime later, she returned. The four of us drove home in complete silence as I tried to understand why I felt so troubled and confused by what had just happened.

What came bubbling up within me were the first stirrings of a disturbing realization that I had been modeling to my daughters the same passivity that my mother had modeled to me as I was growing up at home. What came back to me was a flood of memories of my mother coming to me right after my father had hit me and all the times she would come to me in the morning after I had sat at night at the top of the stairs the night before, listening to my father hitting her or pulling her hair, and hearing my mother telling me, with a sense of urgency in her voice, not to do anything to upset my father.

What gradually became clear to me was that my mother's motto of peace at any price was not worth the price. At the same time, I realized how delicate and challenging it is to step forward in honoring the truth of yourself and others when you have been and perhaps still are traumatized and living in a precarious and potentially life-threatening situation.

What helped me to get through the ongoing, trau-matizing stress of my troubled marriage was the relief I found in continuing to lead weekend contemplative retreats. And so as the stress and sadness of my life at home was in full ongoing crisis mode, I was grateful to lead a weekend contemplative retreat in Orange County, just south of where we lived in Pasadena. On the opening night of the retreat, all the retreatants were in the church listening to the director of the retreat house welcoming them to the retreat. As I waited to be introduced, I was standing in the back of the church, looking over my notes.

Suddenly a woman walked up to me and kissed me on the cheek! I looked up to see Maureen standing there smiling at me! I knew who she was because five years earlier, when I first moved to California to begin my doctoral studies, she was one of the people who began to come to me for spiritual direction. The focus of her spiritual direction sessions was to discern if it was God's will for her leave California to move back to Connecticut to live with her parents so she could attend classes at Saint Joseph College in Hartford, Connecticut, to qualify her to be a spiritual director. She discerned that that was what she was supposed to do. When she left, I felt it was a good decision and assumed it was very unlikely that we would ever meet again. That is why I was so surprised some five years later when she showed up at the retreat in Orange County unannounced, kissing me on the cheek, and taking delight in how surprised I was to see her.

She told me she had completed her program in spiritual direction and was hired as a full-time spiritual director at Holy Spirit Retreat Center, a local retreat house in nearby Southern California, where I also led contemplative retreats. I told her I was happy for her and suggested that after the evening conference I was about to give we could meet in the garden of the retreat house to catch up with each other.

In order for you to appreciate the ways in which our evening walk in the retreat house garden was going to draw both of us into a whole new phase of our healing journey, I must share with you what I knew of Maureen's character, of who I sensed and knew her to be as a person, based on my impressions of her when she was coming to me for spiritual direction some five years earlier. For, you see, so much of who I have come to be as I write these reflections flows from who Maureen was and the ways we sustained and transformed each other in our years together.

Maureen got married right out of high school into a physically abusive marriage. After leaving her marriage, she lived alone, working for a time as a model in New York and then working with a cosmetic company in international sales, flying to major cities around the world to evaluate stores that carried her company's products. During this time she fell into heavy drinking and other destructive behaviors.

When her company moved her from the New York to the Los Angeles office, she began to have blackouts from her drinking. She lost her job and at this low point in her life went into recovery in Alcoholics Anonymous. Her commitment to her recovery renewed her Irish Catholic heritage, which helped her to understand her relationship to her higher power and allowed her to achieve the sobriety she was, by her own efforts, powerless to achieve.

Her spiritual path led her into a training program to become a hospital chaplain, which in turn led her into the charismatic prayer movement, and from there into contemplative prayer, which led her to attend a conference I was giving on Saint John of the Cross's understanding of the dark night of the soul at Mary and Joseph Retreat House in nearby Palos Verdes, California. By the way, after Maureen and I got married, we went together each year to an Advent contemplative retreat, that I gave at that retreat house where we first met. And it was there, together on our last retreat that she awoke in the middle of the night, agitated and confused by the sudden onset of symptoms of dementia from which she would die three years later.

And so with this background information in mind, I can return to Maureen and I beginning our evening walk in the retreat house garden. She started right in by expressing how grateful and amazed she was for her having been offered a full-time position as a spiritual director at a nearby retreat house and for having found a small one-room apartment near the beach where she had always wanted to live.

Her self-disclosures took an unexpected turn as she began to tell me that for the first time in all her years of cherishing her solitude in living alone since her divorce she was beginning to feel lonely. She sensed that God was inviting her to be open to being married again. She told me that she knew in her heart that, should the man she was meant to be with ever come along, he would have to share with her a deep commitment to his own experience and understanding of the spiritual path as the foundational basis of his life.

She showed me the black onyx ring she had always worn on the wedding ring of her left hand ever since her mother had given it to her years ago after her divorce. But just recently she had taken it off the wedding ring finger of her left hand and placed it on her right hand as her way of sending the message out to the universe that she was open to a relationship if that was meant to be.

Moved by her revelations, I told her that I was also going through a time of deep transition in my life. Even though I never imagined my marriage would ever actually end, a recent series of very painful events had led to me to realize that my marriage had become so destructive to my wife and myself and our children that the only honest and healthy thing to do was to face the fact that my marriage was over. My voice was shaking as I heard myself telling her this, because sharing this made my unimaginable situation more real. It was not until months later that Maureen told me that as she slept that night after our talk in the garden she was awakened in her sleep by a voice that told her I was going to be her husband.

At the end of our walk around the garden, she asked if she could resume seeing me for spiritual direction. I said, yes, of course, and told her she could call to make an appointment at the office where I was beginning to see people in supervised psychotherapy and spiritual direction. When she called to make her appointment, she asked if we could be friends. I asked her what she meant. And she said, "You know, friends." I could visit her at her place, where we could walk on the beach, support each other, and talk about our shared commitment to the interior life. I told her that I did not know what to say, but I would think it over and give her my decision when she came to see me for spiritual direction.

When she came to see me for spiritual direction, she was visibly happy when I told her that, in having thought it over, I felt it would be ok for us to spend time together as friends to see how that went. At the end of our session, as she walked past me toward the door to leave, without being aware of what I was about to do, I took her in my arms and kissed her. She kissed me back and said, "Now we know what we know." I walked her down to her car. As we waved goodbye to each other as she drove away, I remember wondering just what it was that we both knew that we knew.

And so, while the nightmare at home dragged on, I would steal away to be with Maureen. Once when Maureen and I were sitting out on the jetty, watching the sailboats going by, I started crying, telling her that I did now know how to do life. That from the time I was very young, life had always seemed to me to be too overwhelming for me to figure out or know how to do it correctly.

I can remember telling Maureen how my wife would sometimes tell me that I had ruined her life. And how I had come to believe that she was right, that I had done her a grave disservice by roping her into getting involved with the likes of me. And how I knew I had let my children down as well in not knowing how to be the father they needed and deserved me to be. Maureen would listen when I talked like this, and she encouraged me to continue doing my best as I kept trying to sort things out.

One day when I was sitting at my desk at home and my wife and youngest daughter were out shopping, my oldest daughter, who was in the midst of her pregnancy, asked if we could talk. Out of the clear blue sky she said, "Dad, if I come to see you ten years from now, you know what I hope for? I hope you are living alone with your books and your icons and we can have a nice visit. Or I hope you find somebody, and you can read a passage out of one of your spiritual books, and she can read a passage out of one of hers. But what I don't want to see is you and Mom together." As she said this, we both teared up. I stood up and hugged her and said I did not want to see that either, for I knew her mother and I were in the grips of a longstanding unhealthy relationship that was hurtful to both ourselves and to her and her younger sister. Inspired by that talk, I moved out of the house and into a room at a nearby retreat house and then into an apartment on nearby Esperanza Avenue, so it would be easy for my daughters to visit.

It was then that I found the courage to hire an attorney to begin formally processing my divorce. I drove from the attorney's office to visit Maureen and told her that I had finally filed for divorce. Less than ten minutes after I told her that I had filed, we made love for the first time. As we were making love, I could feel within myself that I was crossing over into a new phase of my life from which there was no turning back. And I sensed in those moments that Maureen was crossing over, joining me in the beginning of our new life together in which neither one of us wanted a way to turn back and, as our good fortune would have it, no turning back was ever needed.

As Maureen and I spent more and more time with each other, she sat down with me, saying we needed to have an important talk. She told me how grateful she was that God had led us to each other and how terrible she would feel if anything ever happened to our newly emerging relationship. Then she went on to tell me in a tearful and heartfelt way that being with me felt like I was living somewhere else, hidden away in the back of a cave. And that, over and over again, she had to go into that cave to find me, to bring me out, so we could be intimate and vulnerable with other.

She told me that what guided and sustained her in her sobriety was her commitment to rigorous honesty and living by the truth that "half-truths avail us nothing." And in fidelity to those spiritual principles of recovery, she told me that in good conscience she could no longer agree to continue seeing me if I did not go into therapy to get the help I needed to heal from the long-term internalized trauma of my childhood and adolescence. She told me that she had been doing some research, and that she had found a therapist who specialized in the treatment of trauma. And she hoped, for my sake and for our sake, that I would be willing to go into therapy with that person or some other highly qualified clinician.

Because I knew that what she was saying was true and because I did not want to risk losing her, I began my long overdue weekly sessions of psychotherapy. Within a few sessions with my new therapist, I could tell that she knew her way around the world that traumatized people live in. And so for the next four or five years, I committed myself to the challenging and transformative process of healing from the long-term, internalized effects of the trauma I experienced in my childhood and adolescence.

As I was in the midst of my psychotherapy, I led a contemplative retreat in which one of the women attending asked to speak with me in private. She told me the story of the gift she received that released her from the traumatizing forces that had overtaken her life. I am now going to share her story with you and then go on share how the evocative imagery of the gift that set her free helped me to realize that my own unique experience of that same gift would help me to heal from the internalized trauma that had held me in bondage since I was a small child.

When the woman on the retreat and I sat down together, she told me that when she and her husband were young and got married, they were overwhelmed with feelings of sadness and loss when they began to realize that their firstborn son was showing signs of severe autism. Her sense of distress intensified as her son's behavioral and cognitive deficits became more and difficult for her to deal with.

When her son was about five years old, she was referred to a psychiatrist who specialized in helping parents cope with the demands of having a child with special needs. When she called to make an appointment with the psychiatrist, he asked her to bring her son with her for her first session. When she arrived with her son for her first visit, she saw that her son had wet himself. She came into the psychiatrist's office crying, holding her son's hand. The psychiatrist gave her an initial sense of relief in getting her son into a program specifically designed to help children on the autistic spectrum. He then asked her, "What about you? Would you like to see me each week at least for a while to help you regain a sense of confidence in your relationship with your husband and your son?" She gladly accepted his offer and spent about a year coming to see him for regular sessions of psychotherapy that helped her to find her way back to a restored sense of being grounded and present in her own life.

One day she told her therapist that she no longer felt she needed to continue seeing him each week. He told her that he agreed. Then he said, "That being so, I have a gift to give you. And I will give it to you if you can tell me what it is." She spontaneously said, with a sense of surprise and joy in her voice, "My son!"

He said, "Yes, that's right. And now as a practicing Buddhist I must pay homage." He got up, knelt on the floor in front of her, and bowed over and touched his forehead to the floor. She was so moved as she shared this with me that she got up out of her chair, fell to her knees in front of me, and bowed over, touching her forehead to the floor. I was so moved by her story and in seeing her there, that I immediately got up and helped her to her feet and encouraged her to sit down so we could continue our conversation.

She told me that she wanted to share her story with me because she sensed in my presence and in the communal silence and sincerity of the retreatants that the weekend retreat was a delicately orchestrated ritual of silent simplicity that embodied the gift that had so transformed her life when she saw and accepted the gift of her son.

She went on to tell me that as she drove home from that final visit with the psychiatrist an amazing thing happened. The street, the trees, the grass, and the sky overhead became luminous, glowing with a gentle light in which she was empowered to see what the world looks like when seen through the eyes of her soul, now opened in seeing and accepting the gift of her son.

She did not actually tell me this, but I found pleasure in imagining how wonderful that moment must have been when she got home from her fateful final visit with the psychiatrist and for the first time saw the gift of her son, who had been there all along, waiting for her to *see* him and to accept him and love him as her son.

I was so moved by the evocative imagery in this woman's story because it helped me to realize that the spiritual depth dimensions of healing that I was seeking in my own therapy were waiting to be realized in my graced ability to see and accept the gift of my traumatized self, by which I had felt so ashamed and so burdened because of the suffering it had brought into my life.

And so I am now inviting you to join me, whoever you might be, in exploring the ways in which the deep healing that occurred in this woman and also in me has the potential of occurring in each of us as we are interiorly healed and set free in seeing and accepting this gift of which we now speak.

At first and for quite some time we tend not to see this gift of endless liberation because it is hidden away and covered over with the regrets that stir in the traumatized and traumatizing patterns that continue to bring so much suffering into our lives.

It was in this confused and traumatized state that the woman arrived with her son for her first visit with the psychiatrist. And it was in this confused and traumatized state that I began my psychotherapy. Within a few sessions with my therapist an alliance of trust grew between us that allowed me to feel safe enough to tell her what it felt like to be me. I can remember telling my therapist that my worst fear was that it was too late for me. That the intensity of my father's rage had found its way into the innermost center of my being. I feared that his rage had left nothing of me to speak of except the scattered, broken vestiges of myself. Meanwhile, I went about pretending to myself and others that I was a real person and that my life mattered.

As the alliance of trust with my therapist continued to deepen, I was able to accept her guidance in taking rescue missions into the dissociative cave within myself to find and bring out into the open the fragmented, splintered-off aspects of my traumatized self. I could feel the first stirrings of healing occurring within me as I learned to listen to the memories each fragmented aspect of myself shared of terrifying moments that, in the timeless, interior world of the unconscious in which they lived, were as raw and fresh as when these fear-filled moments had actually occurred. Each memory brought with it a tearful confusion that came spilling out of me as I allowed myself to feel and to grieve and to integrate into myself the unfolding story of my own life.

Please understand this was not at all a smooth and easy journey. Sometimes I would get in touch with too much terror all at once, causing the slowly emerging, more grounded sense of myself to become flooded and incapacitated by memories that still held more power than I could endure. But each time this happened, I carried on with the inner work of stepping back to understand and accept that what my therapist was telling me was true: that I really was learning to be skilled in the artistry of this arduous and life-transforming work of reclaiming the foundational sense of myself that I had for long feared was impossible for me to find.

As the layers of my internalized trauma were integrated into broader, more reality-based and empowered dimensions of myself, the ghostlike effigy of myself began to give way to a more substantive and secure sense of wholeness that included and transcended the lost world in which I had been living for so long.

My rescue missions were clearly a gift to the fragmented, traumatized aspects of myself that had for so long been hiding away in the dissociative cave within me. I began to realize how true it is that when love touches suffering, the suffering turns love into mercy. And I was learning to become a merciful person by learning to be merciful toward the traumatized, fragmented aspects of myself.

The expanding effects of the gift of my healing transformations were surely also a gift to Maureen, who had gifted me with her quiet insistence that I get the help that she could see that I needed. And it gifted me to see how gifted she felt herself to be with me in my newfound ability to be lovingly present to her in a vulnerable and intimate manner. And the expanding efficacy of this gift spilled over into my newfound capacity to love and be loved by my two daughters, with whom I had always wanted to be, but did know how to be, as loving and present as they deserved and needed me to be.

All that I have been saying about the cascading gift of love and mercy is true. But what then are we to say of the gift that the psychiatrist saw shining out from the woman that moved him as a practicing Buddhist to kneel before the woman, touching his forehead to the floor? And what are we to say of the gift that the woman received driving home that empowered her to see how the road and trees and grass and sky overhead glowed with the heavenly light she was empowered to see in seeing and accepting the gift of her son?

In each of these instances we can say that the gift is God's merciful presence, cascading down into the lowest and most broken places within ourselves and others, waiting to be seen and trusted so that it might lead us out of the darkness and into the light. It is this gift of God's merciful presence that washed over me when I was three years old, lying alone in the dark, filled with fear and sadness as I listened to my father hitting my mother just outside my bedroom door, sensing how God was so unexplainably merging with me and sustaining me in my sadness and fear. It is this gift of God's merciful presence that sustained me later in all those times I would come to my room to pray after having just sat at the top of the stairs listening to my father raging at my mother. It was the gift of God's merciful presence that moved me to enter the monastery, where the gift of God so mysteriously took me to itself in the loft of the abandoned sheep barn and in chanting the Psalms and in the primordial silence in which God's presence transformed me into itself in ways not for the telling. It was the gift of God's merciful presence that flowed so freely at the Veterans Administration hospital in the initiation rite at the meeting of Alcoholics Anonymous.

The light that shines out from moments such as these sets our hearts aglow with a renewed realization of the ways in which God's merciful presence has brought us up to this very moment in which I am writing these words, this very moment in which you are reading them.

As my time with the woman on the retreat was coming to an end, she told me that within a few weeks after seeing and accepting the gift of her son she went to an art store and bought an easel, brushes, water colors, and paper and set to work with childlike sincerity in attempting to express and share with others something of the gift of God that she saw shining out from the hidden center of all things.

She had brought with her to our session one of her earliest paintings, saying she wanted to give it to me as a gift. I gladly accepted and cherished the gift of that painting of a lone flower rising up from a deep green stem into the bright golden yellow of the blossom. I hung the painting on the wall behind me where I sat with the men and women coming to see me for psychotherapy so that they could see it over my shoulder. I rarely mentioned the painting to anyone or explained to them the story behind it. But I felt and believed that the unseen light shining out from that painting illumined their healing journey, as they learned to find their way to the deep healing that occurs in seeing and accepting the gift of God that flows in the interior recesses of the wounded hurting places within themselves, waiting to be seen, loved, accepted, and shared with others day by day. When I closed down my practice to stay home and take care of Maureen, after she became ill, I brought that painting home with me, where it now hangs and continues to grace my life each time I see it.

May each of us learn to cherish the gifts of divinizing liberation that flow so unexpectedly into our lives in events so blissful or so terrible that they lay us bare to the presence of God that is always there.

Amen. So be it.

11

The Path

The light that shines out from our graced moments of spiritual awakening illumines the path, the way of life in which the deep healing that spirituality brings into our lives is realized. And so, to begin this chapter I invite you to join me in a poetic meditation on the mysterious circular nature of the healing path. This poetic understanding of the path will provide the context for understanding the ways in which *repentance*, *responsibility*, and *mercy* embody the healing energies of the path itself.

To begin the meditation, I invite you to imagine a woman holding her newborn infant son. She is amazed, in a quiet, interior kind of way, by how small her infant is, weighing hardly anything at all. As she gazes into her infant's unknowing eyes, she keenly senses how limited her infant is in so many ways. Her newborn infant cannot feed himself. Nor can he roll over by himself or sit up or stand up and walk about from one place to another. Her infant cannot engage with her in meaningful conversations or chip in and help with the chores. In these and in countless other ways as well her infant son embodies the essence of limit. And yet with the imperial strength with which her infant clasps her extended little finger, like a king holding a scepter, how limitless her infant is in the midst of his limitations. She is left knowing in the deep-down depths of herself that if she were to die in the act of saving the life of her infant, she would die in the truth.

As time goes by, her son goes through the developmental phases in which he emerges in his reflective consciousness of himself as a person—at one with, yet, as time goes by, ever more distinct from his mother as he grows into and finds his way in his own adult life. He goes off to college or maybe not. He gets married or maybe not. He and his wife have a child or two or three or maybe not. And in and through these evolving phases of his passage through time he and his mother are grateful for their ongoing love for each other.

As the years go by, her adult son becomes aware that as his mother grows older, she is becoming increasingly fragile and limited in so many ways. Finally, at long last, he is sitting at his mother's bedside as she lies quiet and still in her final moments of life on this earth. As he sits next to her, listening to her labored breathing, he is moved in the deep-down depths of himself in realizing how strange it is that his mother, who once held him in the limitations of his infancy, has now herself become limited in so many ways. She cannot sit up by herself. She cannot stand up and walk about from one place to another. Nor can she engage with him in one of the loving conversations they have so appreciated over the years. As he gazes into her unknowing eyes, he sadly realizes that she shows no signs of knowing who he is. Nor is there any sign that she remembers who she was in her own life on this earth. In these and in so many other ways as well, he intimately realizes that his mother has become the essence of limit. And yet, with the imperial strength with which she clasps his extended little finger, like a queen holding a scepter, she all but carries his heart away. He knows in the deep-down depths of himself something of the divine dimensions of the mysterious circular nature of our journey through time from birth to death.

To be on the spiritual path is to know that God's limitless presence in our lives is not limited to the momentous moment when our circular journey through time completes itself as our last breath meets and merges with the gift and miracle of our first breath. To be on the spiritual path is to sense within ourselves that what God has revealed to us in the scriptures is true. In knowing this, we sense that God's limitless presence wholly permeates our limitations, guiding us in ever-so-subtle and mysterious ways in each passing moment of our lives.

To be on the spiritual path is to know that love is the overflowing fullness of God's limitless presence, moving us and prompting us to yield to God's loving presence, embodied in our sincere efforts to be as loving as we can be toward God, ourselves, others, and the earth that sustains us all.

And to be on the spiritual path is to know by experience how often the centrifugal force of our circular journey through time sends us flying out and away from our felt sense of interconnectedness with God's presence in our lives. And how this disconnected and harried state is intensified by fear and anger and other painful emotions, rooted in past and present traumas and abandonments, causing us to get caught up in unloving and hurtful beliefs, attitudes, and ways of treating ourselves and others.

It is in the midst of these sad and harried times that the spiritual path becomes the healing path. We learn to discern and accept the promptings of grace to activate the healing energies of *repentance*, *responsibility*, and *mercy*. In doing so, we find our way back to the sense of God's sustaining presence, from which we had strayed in the immaturity and confusion of our wounded and wounding ways.

As I begin to share this phase of my healing journey with you, I can sense Maureen urging me to say, in the language of Alcoholics Anonymous, that we are now beginning to explore the deep healing that occurs in making a fearless inventory of our lives, illumined and guided by the merciful light of our higher power seeing us, loving us, and endlessly taking us to itself in the midst of our limitations.

I will begin by sharing a painful memory from my first marriage. This painful memory that I am about to share with you occurred when I was in my third year of doctoral studies. My wife and I were home alone on a Saturday evening, watching an exquisitely done and moving film entitled *The Mission*. It is about a Jesuit mission in a remote area of South America that served the spiritual and material needs of the Indigenous people who lived in that area.

There were forces at work that were preparing to close the mission. One of the main characters in the film is a priest who led the people in prayer, asking God to help them to preserve the mission. Another key figure in the film is a man who taught the people to use guns to defend the mission. The movie is, in effect, a nuanced exploration of violence and nonviolence as two contrasting ways of responding to injustice.

The movie was personally meaningful to me because it reminded me of Thomas Merton's writings in *Seeds of Destruction* and *Conjectures of a Guilty Bystander,* in which he shared his insights into the spiritual foundations of nonviolence. The film was also personally meaningful to me because the Jesuit priest and social activist Daniel Berrigan, who had visited Merton at the monastery when I was there, appeared in the film.

Everything between my wife and myself seemed fine as we watched the movie in silence, moved by its graphic scenes and musical score. At the end of the movie my wife said in a calm, matter-of-fact voice, that she knew I would be on the side of the priest leading the people in prayer and that she would be encouraging the people to use guns to defend the mission.

For you to understand what happened next, I must first tell you about a framed silk print of Mary and the Christ Child that hung in the hallway just outside the door of the family room in which my wife and I were sitting. What was unusual about this silk print was that Mary and the Christ Child were depicted as Japanese, and they were dressed in bright red traditional Japanese clothing trimmed in gold. Representing Mary and the Christ Child in this way was meaningful to me because it represented what I had learned from Thomas Merton in the monastery in his deep appreciation of the interconnected resonances that exist between the Christian and non-Christian traditions of all the world's great religions. This print was also personally meaningful to me because it was a gift from Father William Johnston, another friend of Thomas Merton, who was a Jesuit priest on the faculty of Sophia University in Japan.

As the movie ended and my wife said in a calm, matter of fact voice that she knew that I would be helping the priest lead the people in prayer and that she would be teaching them to use guns to defend the mission, she stood up and went out into the hallway. She took the silk print of Mary and the Christ Child off the wall, came into the family room where I was sitting, and sent it crashing down over my head! Glass flew everywhere. In the moment of silence that followed I think she was as stunned as I was by what she had just done.

Without saying a word, I stood up, got a wastebasket, knelt on one knee, and began to pick up the broken pieces of glass off the floor. As I did so, I heard a voice within me ask, "What's wrong with this picture?" Right at that moment I was not able to respond interiorly to the question because I had already retreated into the dissociative, traumatized cave within myself, while my exterior bodily self, which my wife could see, went about doing what it needed to do: going through the motions of picking up the glass.

Then, little by little, the fear and sadness of this moment merged with a memory of myself in high school sitting at the top of the stairs, keeping my vigil as I listened to my father, drunk as a loon, raging at my mother. One night he suddenly came out of the kitchen into the hallway near the stairs, where I was sitting just around the corner of the landing of the stairs where he could not see me. He seized hold of a white porcelain statue of Mary that belonged to my mother and smashed it on the floor. The intensity of anger in which my father smashed the statue of Mary on the floor and the intensity of anger in which my wife smashed the framed silk print of Mary and the Christ Child over my head merged as two moments in a timeless traumatizing world in which I had lived as a child and in which I was living in my marriage.

It was not until I left my marriage and was learning in psychotherapy to grieve and to understand and accept my own traumatizing past that I was able to get past myself enough to understand this painful memory from my wife's point of view. I was able to realize that the rage she felt toward me was embodied in the silence in which I was picking up the glass off the floor. For she sensed in my silence and in the images of the movie we had just watched that God was my beloved with whom I was much closer than I was with her, not to mention the closeness she felt existed between me and the people who were coming to my retreats and sharing their own spiritual longings with me in spiritual direction and psychotherapy.

I also came to understand that the move to California for my five years of being absorbed in my doctoral studies had only intensified my wife's sense of feeling unseen and of her own needs unmet in our marriage. Adding to this was that her father had died not long before our move to California, leaving her feeling even more alone in being far from her mother and sister in the familiarity of her childhood home in Ohio.

In speaking in this way, I am not trying to justify anything about her behavior or my own. I am rather trying to understand everything illumined by a sincere sense of repentance for the ways in which my survival strategy of hiding away within my dissociative cave was understandably experienced by her as a kind of abandonment. And how my emotionally distancing passivity triggered her survival strategy of feeling momentarily empowered by her angry outbursts, which in turn intensified my survival strategy of hiding yet deeper within the cave of myself. This dynamic left us both caught in a vortex of deepening feelings of abandonment, anger, and fear that neither one of us was able to understand or respond to in ways that might have saved our marriage.

As a final note to this story, it is important for me to add that my wife had the silk print of Mary and the Christ Child matted and reframed in a beautiful gold frame. It meant the world to me when she gave it to me, because I saw in her gesture an expression of sincere repentance. When I looked at that silk print, I was especially touched by a small crease and tear in one corner of the silk print, where it had been cut by glass when she broke the print over my head. For me, that crease and tear embodied the opening through which the mercy of God shines out through our sincere repentance for the wounded and wounding things we as human beings sometimes do to one another.

Repentance is then much deeper than simply regretting the suffering our behavior has caused to ourselves and others. For we might regret what we have done simply because we got caught or because our hurtful behavior threatens our positive image of ourselves in our own eyes and in the eyes of others. Nor is repentance a harsh, self-condemning response to our inability to overcome the particularly entrenched habits of our minds and hearts that perpetuate suffering. For there is a quality of mercy inherent in the deep healing that repentance brings into our lives as we learn to sense how God's merciful love is incarnate in our own merciful love for ourselves and others, in our shared weakness as human beings, and in our commitment to overcome the hurtful habits of our minds and hearts.

In my psychotherapy and with Maureen's help I was able to realize that my newfound sense of repentance mingled with mercy was of little help if I was not willing to take *responsibility* to do everything in my power to transform my spirituality from a way to hide from others into ways of experiencing God's presence empowering me to engage emotionally with Maureen, my two daughters, and those who wanted to be my friends.

I am introverted and reserved in my temperament, as was Maureen. We shared a deep respect for our solitary soulful nature and so Maureen was not expecting me, nor would she have wanted me, to be untrue to our shared introverted nature by blurting out all my thoughts and concerns. The core issue for her was needing to know that when she was sharing some concern or insight, I was truly present and interiorly engaged with her as she spoke. And she needed to know that I sincerely wanted to share the blessings and struggles that were going on within me in our daily life together. By the same token, my daughters needed to know that when I asked how they were doing, I was not doing so out of a social expectation of what I, as their father, was supposed to do. Rather, it was because I really wanted to know how they were doing, because I loved and cared about them as I knew that they loved and cared about me.

It was easy for me, in my role as a spiritual director and a psychotherapist, to be genuinely present and engaged with others as they shared their struggles and concerns. The challenge for me was being emotionally engaged with others when I was just my ordinary day-to-day self. For the intimate immediacy of being with Maureen and my daughters in the details of daily living was too disturbingly similar to how vulnerable and exposed I felt in my ordinary experience of myself in my childhood and adolescence. In those days the only way I could survive the overwhelmingly painful things my father did to me was to hide in the dissociative cave within myself, where I was sustained by God in intimate and unexplainable ways.

And so I found it very difficult to free myself from my longstanding survival strategy of feeling safe by knowing how to trick Maureen, my two daughters, and fellow students in my doctoral program into thinking I was right there talking to them, when in reality, without their knowing it, I had already retreated into the dissociative cave where no one but God could find me. As I kept slipping again and again into the emotionally distancing habits, from which I was sincerely trying to free myself, I caught myself feeling ashamed and impatient with the still-traumatized and fear-based aspects of myself that needed to be loved the most.

It was in listening to and being with the men and women coming to me for psychotherapy and spiritual direction that I came to realize that it is never easy for us to see and to accept how powerless we are to break free of the habits of our minds and hearts that cause suffering to ourselves and others. The litany of these wounded and wounding patterns goes on and on: fear-based passivity and isolation from others, resentments, being quick to anger, narcissistic entitlement, neglecting to nurture and honor the spiritual dimensions of ourselves and others, all forms of prejudice, sexually exploitative behavior or withholding intimacy from a committed partner who simply wants to love us, feelings of self-loathing, and so on. If your personal wounded and wounding pattern was not mentioned in the above list, you can add it now.

It is in experiencing and accepting how difficult it can be to free ourselves from our hurtful attitudes and ways of treating ourselves and others that we begin to understand that the healing path is not a linear process in which we can force our way beyond our wounded and wounding ways. Rather, it is a path along which we learn to circle back again and again to cultivate within ourselves a more merciful understanding of ourselves as we learn to see, love, and respect the still-confused and wounded aspects of ourselves. Insofar as these wounded and wounding aspects of ourselves recognize that they are seen, loved, and respected in such a merciful way, they can feel safe enough to release the pain they carry into the more healed and whole aspects of ourselves.

We are now attempting to bear witness to the sweet secret of experiential salvation in which the torn and ragged edges of our wounded and wayward hearts are experienced as being like that tear in the silk print of Mary and the infant Jesus: the opening through which the gentle light of God's merciful love shines into our lives.

Each religion has its own way of expressing the divine dimensions of merciful love. In my own Christian tradition the divine mercy flowing into our lives is embodied in our faith in Jesus, in whom it is revealed that God's response to us is to become identified with us as invincibly loved and one with God in the midst of our dilemma. In Christ it is revealed that God does not withhold his love until we measure up to being the awake, caring, and loving persons we are called to be. To the contrary, we see in Christ how God seeks us out, accesses us, and draws us in ever closer to God in the midst of our wayward ways, even as we continue to stumble and fall this way and that. And even as we continue to stumble, we discover that we are falling again and again into the depths of the merciful love of God, which is lifting us up and carrying us forward in unexplainable ways.

Years ago a woman attending one of my weekend contemplative retreats shared with us that when her mother was in the final stages of a terminal illness, she gathered her children around her bed for a preplanned ritual in which she would give to each child the pieces of her jewelry that she hoped they could cherish after her death.

The woman told us that when she and her siblings had gathered, they helped their mother to sit up in bed and placed her jewelry box on her lap. In a sincere and ceremonial way their mother began to give each piece of jewelry to each child until finally she said, "There, I am finished."

The woman told us that she saw one piece of jewelry, an emerald ring, was still left in the box. Lifting the ring out of the box, she told her mother, "Look, Mom, you are not quite finished. There is still this emerald ring." At which point her mother took the ring out of her hand and said, "I just got that ring. I am not giving that up."

Even as she was being carried away in the depths of God, her mother was not able to comprehend and yield to the immensity and mystery of her death. But what got to me was not the image of the woman's mother, lying dead in bed still clutching that emerald ring. Rather, it was the way in which her daughter was moved in telling us that in that moment her mother was all the more lovable to her in revealing how human she was. And I sensed in the woman's merciful, tearful sharing of the beauty she saw in her mother's limitations a trace of how God sees us: all the more lovable in our limited capacity to see our limitations shining bright with the limitless mercy of God.

In my years with Maureen I was able to make amends with my two daughters for the ways I was not there for them just when they needed me the most. I am so proud of who they have become and so grateful for the love we share and how they keep close tabs on me in my declining years. When we are having a glass of wine together over a meal, as we raise our glasses for a toast, we say together, "To the path." The path, of course, being the healing path we have been exploring together in these reflections.

The most all-pervasive transformative grace of my ongoing healing journey has been the quiet, sensual, prayerful bliss that Maureen and I shared together over the years in simple rituals of circling about one another in an ongoing soulful communion. Two reclusive Irish Catholics with Buddhist tendencies living here together at the edge of the sea.

When I chose the mysterious circular nature of the healing path as the overarching metaphor of this chapter, I was not consciously aware that these reflections have been following a circular journey of their own, in which the concluding words of this final chapter are about to come full circle in meeting and merging with the opening words of the Introduction, which I began to share with you a little over two years ago.

At a yet more intimate level, when I began this chapter with the poetic imagery of the mother and her infant in their vast circular journey from birth to death, I was not consciously aware of how the imagery of their story so deeply resonates with the opening words of the Introduction, which I wrote while sitting next to Maureen as she was dying right here in this room in which I am now sitting. And this leads me to wonder if it is not so that in the deep-down interiority of ourselves, we know much more than we consciously realize concerning the mysterious and ultimately divine dimensions of our lives together on this earth. And wondering, too, if it is not so that the wisdom dimensions of the healing path of our unfolding lives through time can be best understood as the ways we are quickened from within, in often unexpected ways, by deepening intimations of what we have perhaps always known, hidden with Christ in God from before the origins of universe.

May each of us, at our own pace and in our own unique way continue to deepen our heartfelt trust in knowing that God, who is the origin, sustaining ground, and fulfillment of our healing journey, will and already is bringing the healing journey of our lives to completion.

So it is that I end these reflections in the evening of Pentecost Sunday, June 5, 2022.

Amen. So be it.